SONGS
OF A
WAR
BOY

SONGS
OF A
WAR
BOY

DENG THIAK
ADUT

with BEN MCKELVEY

H hachette
AUSTRALIA

hachette
AUSTRALIA

Published in Australia and New Zealand in 2016
by Hachette Australia
(an imprint of Hachette Australia Pty Limited)
Level 17, 207 Kent Street, Sydney NSW 2000
www.hachette.com.au

10 9 8 7 6 5 4

Adut, Deng Thiak, author.
Songs of a war boy/Deng Thiak Adut with Ben Mckelvey.

978 0 7336 3652 3

Adut, Deng Thiak.
Child soldiers – Sudan – Biography.
Refugees – Sudan – Biography.
Refugees – Australia – Biography.

Mckelvey, Ben, author.

355.008309209624

Cover design by Christabella Designs
Front cover images courtesy Getty Images; © Telegraph Media Group Limited 2015/David Blair;
author cover photograph by Melissa Mai
Back cover photograph of Deng at a camp when he was a child soldier supplied by the author
Inside front cover image © Telegraph Media Group Limited 2015/David Blair
Inside back cover artwork by Nick Stathopoulos (*Deng*; acrylic and oils on linen 137 × 137 cm)
Map design by Christabella Designs
Text design by Bookhouse, Sydney
Typeset in 12/19.8pt Sabon LT Pro by Bookhouse, Sydney
Printed and bound in Australia by McPherson's Printing Group

Pity the nation that is full of beliefs and empty of religion.

Pity the nation that wears a cloth it does not weave and eats a bread it does not harvest.

Pity the nation that acclaims the bully as hero, and that deems the glittering conqueror bountiful.

Pity the nation that despises a passion in its dream, yet submits in its awakening.

Pity the nation that raises not its voice save when it walks in a funeral, boasts not except among its ruins, and will rebel not save when its neck is laid between the sword and the block.

Pity the nation whose statesman is a fox, whose philosopher is a juggler, and whose art is the art of patching and mimicking.

Pity the nation that welcomes its new ruler with trumpeting, and farewells him with hooting, only to welcome another with trumpeting again.

Pity the nation whose sages are dumb with years and whose strongmen are yet in the cradle.

Pity the nation divided into fragments, each fragment deeming itself a nation.

– Kahlil Gibran, *The Garden of the Prophet*

To my mum, Athieu Akau Deng,
aka youhyouh, my galaxy.

And to my brother, John Mac, who rescued me.
Everything I do is to make your sacrifices worthwhile.

CONTENTS

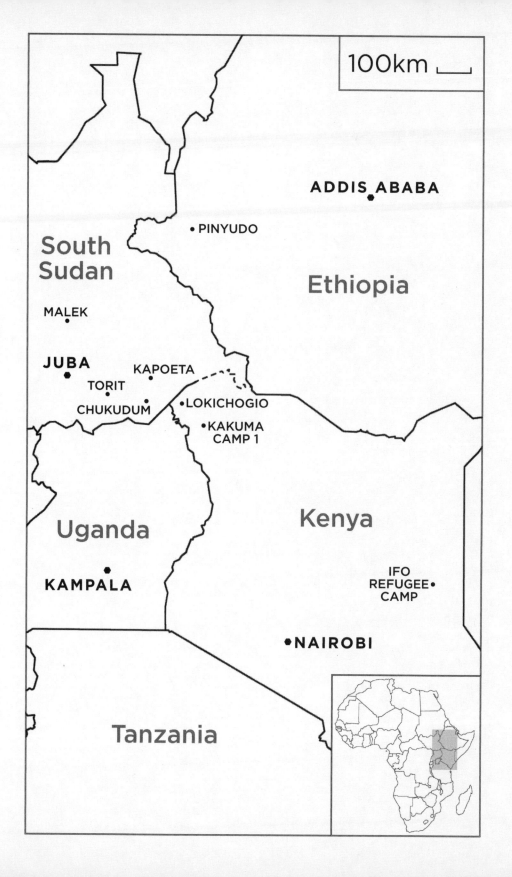

FOREWORD

I was in my late thirties when I first went to South Sudan – a man neither green nor easily over-awed. For more than a decade I had reported on conflict and upheaval, massacres and calamity, but it turned out I was not as seasoned as I had imagined. Nothing has changed me as profoundly as that first journey into Dinka lands.

It was 1998, a time of war and famine. I found my way to northern Bahr el Ghazal, to a frontline village where the dead and dying lay in the dust, alone and untended. Children died at my feet. Their last breaths and the eyes of their mothers are with me today.

South Sudan was a place where people died or were driven mad.

We had flown in from northern Kenya in a single-engine Cessna. The pilot was a New Zealander. At a place called Panacier, in a landscape littered with death, something in the pilot cracked. Before we took off for the final leg back to Kenya, he began sobbing and shouting nonsensically. He ran here and there without purpose. He appeared enraged. Cameraman Steve Levitt and I watched the pilot with concern. His shirt was foaming with sweat.

Finally, he sat behind the controls, crying. As the Cessna clawed into the super-heated African air, without warning he tipped the aircraft over and plunged it towards the ground. He pulled out, the aircraft shuddering, at the level of the trees. Regaining height, he tipped the plane over on the other wing and again we were spearing towards the earth. I waited for death. But again, he pulled out of the dive in the final moment. Two desperately wounded men were lying in the cargo space behind the final seat. One groaned. No one else said anything. Some hours later, we landed near the Red Cross hospital at Lokichogio, unloaded the casualties and never saw the pilot again.

The following year, Levitt and I returned to Sudan with some activists to buy slaves. Our story helped prove the ancient trade was thriving again in conditions made possible by the war.

These reports gained the notice of the small South Sudanese refugee population in Sydney. I was invited to their gatherings. It was here I met John Mac Acuek, who would become one of my greatest friends. We were partners in many endeavours, in charities that he launched and businesses that he floated. He was funny and kind, determined and brilliant. In his every great success and in his many setbacks and disappointments, John always had a new plan and a willingness to bring you in on it. I loved John unreservedly. He was my Mandela. I will not say more about him here. His spirit and his story are in these pages.

On my first visit to John's home in Sydney's Blacktown, he introduced me to a lad he called David. This was Deng. He was just a teenager then, athletic, intense and brooding. He did not say much. He did not know much English. He wore his hair in short, tight spirals and could easily have been a model or the more outlaw kind of soul singer. He radiated charisma. But where his older brother was easy-going and full of charm, Deng struck me as wary. I felt his alienation, his lack of trust. I sensed the great ache of his loneliness.

That Deng has become the man he is today is a miracle, but one of his own making. In the libraries where he lost himself, he unlocked a striking intellect. In the law, he found a moral code to cleave to, a source of dignity and power. It is impossible, on meeting him now, not to be in awe of him. And that is before you know where he has been.

This book tells that story. Here you meet Deng on his own path. It would be unbelievable, were it not true. At the heart of it is a story about who we all are. And what we owe to each other.

Hugh Riminton
Sydney, 2016

PROLOGUE

Songs are of great importance to my people, the Dinka. They're our avatars, and our biographies. They precede us, introduce us and live on after we die. They are also how our deeds escape our villages, and they pass on our code of morality, culture and law.

When I was a boy I dreamed of having my own songs, but now I am a man, and I have no songs. It's likely I never will, in the traditional sense. For the Dinka, these songs are only for men. In the eyes of my culture, I am still a boy.

When I should have been going through the rituals of manhood, I was caught in a vicious war. By the time I was returned to my people, I was very much a westerner.

My feet straddle the continents, and also the threshold of manhood.

I never completed the rites of passage that are required to become a Dinka man, and so in the eyes of some of my people I am half made. I am also half made in the estimation of some Australians too – those who cannot accept me as their countryman because of the darkness of my skin, where I started my life, and my accented English.

I know I am whole, though. Yes, I've had a difficult life. I'm proud of some of the things I have done, and ashamed of others, but I own all of it, and I've reconciled with all of it. That's why I am whole.

Perhaps this book could be my songs.

I came to this country with almost no English, fresh physical and mental scars, and an education that didn't extend much farther than the ability to strip and clean an AK-47 rifle. About a decade and a half later, I have my own law firm.

I'm still a relatively young man, but I think perhaps I have done a few things that deserve song. In Africa, I've hunted and killed, and survived bombardment and disease. I've charged headlong at machine-gun posts. I've been taken to the mouth of death many times, and have always been lucky enough to be able to pull myself out.

In Australia, I became educated, and also became a man of standing in my community. I once thought that finishing my law degree, and my master's, would be the greatest achievements of my life, but I've found a much-needed home in law and I've gone on to accomplishments that have benefited not just myself, but others. I'm especially proud of the work I've done with my dispossessed African brothers and sisters. Would any of it be worthy of song? I think so.

I've been able to adorn myself with fine things too, which is an important rite for the Dinka. I have my suits made for me so they fit perfectly, and I have European watches and fine-smelling leather boots and bags.

To go to South Sudan and look at us, the Dinka, with western eyes, you may assume that we are a people who do not value finery, but that's not the case. Though we have no need for diamonds or designer clothes in Africa, the acquisition of a fine looking cow, or a hand-hammered cowbell, or handmade spear, or of a leopard-skin to wear when wrestling is very important to a Dinka man. If we own luxury items that are honestly earned, then they must be represented in our songs, too. My suits would not have their own songs, but they could certainly bring flavour to some of my verses.

Perhaps my songs could also be songs for the other boys who were taken from their villages and mothers, and for those scarred, confused black men that you see in the outer suburbs of western cities; their looks of fear often mistaken for anger.

Ideally every war boy should be able to sing their own songs, but so many are dead, and so many who have survived have no voice. Even though I hesitate to collectively recognise my brothers, I feel that any one of them who wants to share my verses should be able to do so because there should be songs for everybody, even the war boys.

The chapters in this book are the verses of my songs. The songs of Deng Thiak Adut, the songs of a war boy.

Chapter One

THE VILLAGE OF THE GOD EATER

I was born lucky. I was born as part of a large family, and amidst a strong tribe. We are the Dinka-Bor – that is the name that's mostly used for us. There is another name for us, but that name is too formidable to be used much. Some names, like some songs, are too powerful for their own good.

I will say it here, once, but I will say it softly. We are the Mony Jieng – the 'men of humanity'.

I was born into a village that was not built for us Dinka-Bor, but for our long-horned cattle, which are sacred to my people. The cattle bless the body, the land and the

1

soul. They would die without us, and we would not be Dinka-Bor without them.

I was born amidst the cattle in a *luak*, a grass-made cattle shed near a village called Malek. A family of swallows watched on as one woman struggled, and others offered gentle encouragement. I took some of the soul of one of the birds as I took my first breaths, and in doing so I also took their name: *Aolouch* or Little Swallow.

Little Swallow was also born with more status. The mother who birthed me, Athieu Akau Deng, was the most recently betrothed of my father's six wives. As the last wife, she was the first among equals in clan estimation. The women whom my father had previously married were also my mothers, but they were not Athieu Akau Deng. Athieu Akau Deng had status, reputation, but also poise and wisdom.

Athieu means 'born with a struggle', Akau means 'support and fealty', and Deng means 'god of the rain'. All names speak to who my mother of mothers is.

In my village, my father, Thiak Adut Garang, was considered a prosperous man. He was a fisherman, but also had a banana farm, and owned many heads of cattle, all of whom he could recognise at a glance.

If a man wished to marry a woman like my mother, he needed to own a great herd.

My mother's clan – the Dinka-Adol – are known for having some of the most powerful women in all the Dinka lands, and my mother was tall and strong, even when standing next to her tribeswomen. I do not know what my father paid for her, but it would have been quite a stampede.

Athieu Akau Deng is still a powerful woman, although now she's an old woman, so bears her power in her eyes, not her body.

My father was alive when I was born, but not when I started to take on memories. He died of old age, which was the way many people used to die in my village.

I knew my father mostly because of the songs men sung about him – with the finest being a tale of when he hunted a hippopotamus with his spear, and fed the entire village for days.

Tradition dictated that his grave was next to our *luak* and I would often think about him when I walked past it. In our village, men were the exclusive holders of male wisdom, so my mothers couldn't tell me the stories of my father, but my brothers, some of who had spent twenty or thirty years with him, would spend long afternoons singing his songs and telling his stories.

My father was a great hunter and fisherman, my brothers would tell me. He was a fighter too, apparently. Our tribe had long been in a simmering conflict with another clan called the Palek and there was a story that I especially enjoyed that culminated in my father throwing a Palek warrior into a burning pile of cow dung. I liked to hear that story over and over, waiting with bated breath for the buttock-burning conclusion, which would always put me in fits of laughter.

My brothers would tell me that, after the chief (a position that rotated around the four most powerful families in the village), my father was one of the most respected men in our part of the world. The weight of his name, Thiak, was considerable, and as the eldest surviving son of my father's last wife, it is mine. Of all of my names, it is the one I am perhaps most proud of and the fact that that name is now on the cover of this book makes me immeasurably proud.

There was another piece of great fortune that was handed to me when I was born, and that was that my mother gave birth next to the White Nile River, an endless brown–green band flowing south to north that deserves tribute from all who are alive, man or beast. There is no life without the Nile, and no Nile without rain. The God of Rain, Deng, is one of the most powerful deities in our world. For the Dinka, life comes and goes on the ebb of Deng's mood.

My first memories are of the creatures that came to the Nile to hunt or drink. I especially loved the large Nile eagles, which would soar high over the river, as though they were the fingers of a dancing man, before carving through the air, smashing into the water, and emerging with a catfish struggling between the sharp points of their claws.

To be able to simply reach into the brown of the water and bring out food like that was powerful magic as far as I was concerned. I knew men like my father could pull food from the river too, but for them it seemed like toil. It was no more effort for the Nile eagle to fish than it was for the sun to plod across the sky each day.

One of my first fully formed memories was of a clash between two Nile eagles. One had pinched a fat, glistening fish from the river, and the other had attempted to steal his friend's quarry. Their claws locked mid-air and they spiralled down, as though both suddenly wingless.

The eagles landed heavily in front of Ayuen Kon, one of my mothers, who was sitting with me near the river. I felt the hurt in the animals' bodies when I heard their landing. Even as an infant, I understood that animals that lived in the sky did not need to have heavy bones, or tough skin.

My mother approached the eagles, which were chirping mournfully and quietly. Their claws were still locked, and the eagles no longer had the strength to extricate themselves from the combative embrace. Ayuen spoke to the large birds softly and I was stunned to find that the eagles allowed her to pull their claws apart. Eagles are not like dogs, and usually do not listen to what humans have to say.

When free from each other, the animals walked around slowly, but could not fly.

'Fly! Fly!' I said in hushed tones.

My longing for the birds to be in the sky again was perhaps my first desire. I had needs before, but remember no earlier desires.

My mother disappeared towards our hut, returning with a gourd of water. She poured some drops into each animal's beak. That seemed to calm them. They were still for some minutes, until one bird postured, spread its wings, let out a cry and took to the sky. Its friend watched for a moment, and then followed up and away. After a few wheeling moments above the river, both eagles disappeared from view.

I watched the spot where I'd last seen the birds and I wondered how I would feel if I suddenly found myself stuck up in the sky. I stared at the sky for some time afterwards, long past the length of my mother's patience. I stared and stared and thought about flying, until I was called to eat.

It was a rare event that I had to be called to eat.

I was only *Aolouch* until I was *Acham-Nhialic*. It was a nickname given to me when, one day, I lay on my back with some of my brothers and mused out loud that if I could catch and kill *Nhialic*, the big god who was made out of the sky, we would have enough food for the entire village to eat. More than that, I continued in the stunned silence, there would be leftovers forever.

For a minute my brothers mused on whether there was more power in the blasphemousness or hilarity of what I had said. It seemed that laughter won the day and from that moment I was called *Acham-Nhialic* or the God Eater.

In my very young years, almost all of the trouble in my life stemmed from my insatiable stomach. I would cry and whine at night if, at the end of the day, my belly wasn't as full as the river after the rains. If there was food in the pot, I would always be trying to cram fish or *ugali* (a delicious dough made of maize flour and water) in my mouth – even if I was full and the food was just tumbling out of my crammed mouth and onto the floor.

I was a greedy child.

When there was a great kill – an antelope, or a crocodile, or perhaps even a hippopotamus – the meat was distributed according to family status. As a child I had no rights to any of the great kill meat, except that which my mothers or brothers would give to me. Often, however, I would eat better than some of the adults as it was easier to feed me than listen to my whining.

I often thought gristly antelope meat was a meagre consolation for one who wished to eat the biggest god of them all, but I would never refuse food, regardless of what it was.

I remember one afternoon deciding to chew on some scattered cornhusks that had been tossed on the ground, which were also being enjoyed by a troop of wild baboons. When the monkeys and I had finished our meal, I decided we were compatriots, so I led them through our gate and into our *luak* so we could all search for another course together.

When one of my mothers came into the *luak* and discovered a barrel of monkeys and a gluttonous fat little child sharing the precious fresh corn supplies, well, there was wrath enough for both species.

I was suspicious of the baboons after that day. They had tricked me, and when I saw them, I looked at them with narrowed eyes.

One day some of my brothers and I made a bow and arrows to shoot at the larger bugs and beetles near the river. After seeing how true the arrows flew, I decided I would get even with those monkeys that had caused my buttocks to be whipped.

I waited for two of the baboons to engage in an act that I didn't understand, but I knew to be private. Then I let loose with an arrow, right at the point where their simian bodies met. I hit the male baboon. He reared up in outrage, and then instantly identified his assailant. He sized me up and made me as an opponent of manageable size.

The baboon ran at me, screeching a song of violence. He was fast, but, moving with both hands and feet, he couldn't really attack me until he sat down. When he did, I would dart away from him. It was a high stakes game of tag that I started to understand could have very painful repercussions.

I was saved once again by a mother, and once again my bottom felt an angry mother's wrath.

The time that my stomach led me to the gravest danger was down at the Nile, where I used to play with a couple of village girls named Akuol and Nyandit. The three of us used to wade into the water, at the mouth of an irrigation tunnel, and there I would try to catch, with my hands, any fish unlucky enough to travel through the tunnel.

When I would manage to grab a fish, I would bite into its belly, spitting out the skin, scales and bones, and swallowing the delicious pink–white flesh. I thought the only danger in that game was that escaped fish would sometimes bite my testicles but there was another greater danger. I didn't know that some fish were not tasty and nourishing. I didn't know that some fish had flesh that would attack my stomach with a thousand knives.

I was sick for weeks after eating that evil fish. I could not eat, could not move, and there were concerns that I would be joining my father under a mound next to the *luak*. I survived, but those weeks were the closest I'd been to dying until the war came to our village.

For the first part of my life I knew the village, my family, the Nile and the animals around it, and almost nothing else. I didn't know of the war, because that was something that happened in *madina*s – cities or towns – not villages, like mine. Then the war grew and moved and strange, unfathomable things started happening, one after another.

The first such happening was when I saw a convoy of rumbling vehicles. I had seen a vehicle before – a man in the village had once used a large vehicle that was all wheels and seat to plough a field. I didn't know that there was more than one vehicle in the world though, let alone all these trucks, bouncing along on the hardened mud.

Alongside these vehicles were men wearing cloth on their bodies and legs. I'd never seen that before either. To add to my confusion, these men had lighter skin than the people of the village, and they all held shiny sticks.

I was intrigued but also scared of these men and their vehicles and shiny sticks. The men sang songs that I didn't understand. I later found out that the songs were fierce, about a powerful god called Allah, who I suspected could not be eaten.

Of all my brothers perhaps the closest to me then was a fully grown man named Adut. Despite the age difference, we were particularly fraternal because he and I shared the curse of stammering.

I asked Adut about the men I had seen down at the banks and he looked at me as though he was trying to explain something very complex to me in simple terms.

'T-t-t-here is a north, and i-i-i-t is bad,' Adut told me. 'Those men you saw, *they* are b-b-b-bad.'

I knew nothing of the north then. I didn't know of the Arabs, or of sharia law. Initially, the men were exciting to me. They represented an adventure.

After I saw those men, Adut and some of the other men from the village disappeared, returning with strangers – familiar looking strangers, but strangers nonetheless. These strangers had shiny sticks too, and were always asking for food and water. They were blunt and abrupt about their needs, and I could tell they annoyed the mothers.

There was a collective name for these men and it was Anyanya, which literally translates into 'snake poison'. The Anyanya were fighters, but not fighters like the men who wrestled in my village for bragging rights or status, and not even the men who fought the Palek. These men were in a fight that made them harder, meaner, and gave them marks on their faces, and holes in their bodies.

Adut went off with these Anyanya once, and came back with a hole in his shoulder that made his arm all but useless.

Then, one day, I saw my first machine of war. It was an old tank, which was sitting in one of my uncle's fields. It looked like a metal house, with a beak. I asked my uncle where he got such a thing and he said that he and the Anyanya had killed the men in it and dragged it to the village. I asked if the tank was still alive, but he said it wasn't.

I wondered what my uncle would do with this metal house. My answer came some weeks later when I saw people working in the fields with new metal hoes, shovels and rakes, some bearing markings unique to the tank, and some still bearing the burn marks from the Anyanya attack.

The signs of war came before the danger. When the danger first came, it came in the form of a realised myth.

I had always thought the story of the *nyanjuan* – female werewolves who feasted on the flesh of children – was a fiction made up by adults to keep their little ones from venturing too far into the bush, but when my cousin Makaroau Deng was attacked by one I knew they were real. Deng escaped with just facial mutilation, but when he described the attack later, it was obviously the work of a *nyanjuan*.

I soon saw the *nyanjuan* with my own eyes, prowling around on the edge of the village. They looked just like hyenas, but their eyes were wilder, and their growls were evil, and I could tell that they were far more dangerous than hyenas.

Of course I now know that there is no such thing as a *nyanjuan*. I now know that what I saw were just hyenas turned desperate – their feeding patterns interrupted by the bombs and guns. They had resorted to eating the flesh of the abundant dead bodies nearby, and sometimes children like Makaroau Deng.

The Anyanya came to the village more and more as the war expanded. We fed them, and housed them, and let them rest when they had holes in their bodies or when they were sick. More men from the north came closer and closer to us also.

There was a missionary school in the nearby town of Mading, which hosted people who were teaching writing and reading in a language called English. If you could read this language then you could read a powerful magic book called the Bible. The men from the north hated that book, the language and the town.

Those who could read that book were very good spies apparently, and the men from the north were scared of the spies, so I heard that they killed and killed in that town with nooses and fire and machetes and with the shiny sticks.

One of my older brothers, John, went to that town and learned about the Bible. He had not been born with the name John, but the people who taught him about that magic book told him he had to take a name from the book and get rid of his old name. His old name was Bench Mach, which means 'god of fire'. His new name was the name of one of the men who wrote the magic book.

John used to tell me about the stories in the magic book but they sounded unbelievable to me. I told John that his god didn't know much about life on the Nile. That used to make John very angry.

There were a number of times that John's religion put him at odds with many of the rest of us. There was one instance when, after learning about some things called 'graven images', he decided he was going to burn some of the wooden statues of our Dinka gods. The mothers were very upset with John's vandalism, but people in the village generally did not mind the Christians like John, and understood that they did strange things sometimes.

People were inquisitive about John's god who claimed to have powers like lightning, summoning and resurrection. They reasoned that they might need his help against the encroaching Arabs.

John said that his god had told him he had to go away to fight the Arabs, so he left the village with another brother of mine named Adut Malieth. When I asked people where they had gone, I was told they had gone away to become something called an officer, which was confusing because John had told me he wanted to be a soldier.

One day – maybe when they had finished killing the people in Mading – the Arabs had a fight with the Anyanya near our village. When the fighting started, in between the sounds of roaring thunder, I could hear a lot of yelling in a language I didn't understand. The fighting started in the day, and when the sun went down the fighting continued, on and on.

At night the fighting looked like nothing I had seen before. Lights, like stars but much brighter, flew backwards and forwards, with some of the lights flying across the river and over our village with a sound that was like breaking wood. My little cousins and I were so engaged with the show, we decided to move to a *luak* close to the river so we could get a better view.

When my birth mother found us, huddled near the river, eyes full of tracers, shells and bullets, she yelled at us with a real fury.

'It is dangerous, you stupid boys!' she shouted at us. 'Do you want to be killed?'

I didn't move. I didn't know what it was to be killed, but I knew that I wanted to watch the show. After being dragged to safety, my buttocks were again whipped.

For some time after the battle the men from the north would come to our fields to burn our food and do something else called rape which, I was told, was worse than burning our food. I couldn't imagine what could have been worse than burning our food, but the mothers certainly hated it.

Sometimes, however, there were long periods when the war was happening elsewhere. Sometimes it didn't seem that there was a war at all. The only conflict I saw in those periods was the men who faced off in wrestling matches. That happened when one had questioned the other's manliness. I liked the wrestling. The men would fight with ferocity and then when one wrestler had forced the other to touch the ground, establishing himself as a greater man than the other, both would have to acknowledge the new order of things.

Even in the quiet times I remembered the war, though. Especially when I saw men in the village with holes in them.

I knew the war would be coming back, and I wondered what form it would take when it did.

I could never have envisioned the war's new face, which was announced by my cousin – a deaf boy named Deng Yar who was a little younger than me. One morning he broke the calm of the early hours by running around the village, yelling his mangled, consonant-less words that no one could understand.

I understood them this time though. He was saying 'Beware, beware.'

He was pointing to the sky, but not to any particular point. He was pointing at the entire expanse of blue. We all looked up, but there was nothing to see. There was sky, and some clouds, but there were not even any birds to see . . . until there was a bird, but a very strange one. Most birds glide, like a fish in the water, but this one walked like a man in the middle of a long journey.

The not-bird came closer and closer. Some of the other children had gathered around us. None of us knew what this was in the sky, except, apparently, Deng Yar. He was wailing, agitated and scared, his hands jerking around, palms first, in an awkward dance of fear.

My adrenaline was rising, but I didn't run until the first bombs started landing. The bombs did not land close to me, but their report shook my insides. Through the thunder and the fire and the smoke, frantic mothers collected their children and ran for the river, and the relative safety of the other side. We were lucky; we had a canoe, but many had to swim across the river to the marshes on the other bank.

From the other side, we first watched the northerners attack the village from the sky, and then later we watched them attack us from the ground, after they piled out of trucks. They shot their small guns and big guns at the village and the marshes. There was metal and fire spitting at us, and it was chopping down the trees and the people. Then, it all stopped.

Some of the villagers went back across the water immediately, and some waited hours, days or even weeks. The dead were buried and, for those who were not killed or wounded, life continued in the village, for the most part, as it had before.

The northerners came back, time and time again. As we hid in the marshes, my cousins and brothers would try to figure out what the Arabs had come for. Did they want grain? Did they want our sheds? Had they come for the cows? Had they come for the river?

Eventually, we figured that they had just come to kill us, and that they had no other reason to be in our village. We were children and had no understanding of the politics of war, but we were not far from the truth.

The mothers were careful to make sure the dead were buried without the children seeing the bodies. I wished once again that it was possible to eat the big god *Nhialic*, not because I wanted to fill my belly, but because I wanted to get rid of the sky and the fire-bringing beasts that now lived there.

And then, one day, the northern army stopped having the run of our village. Their planes and trucks and men had fire and metal thrown at them by the Anyanya ... only they weren't the Anyanya anymore, they had become something more dangerous, organised and effective. The Anyanya had joined a new army – the Sudanese People's Liberation Army (SPLA).

The SPLA was just as much of a burden on the village as the Anyanya had been, demanding food, shelter and medical help, but at least they were fighting the northerners with big guns and strong men. Even through a child's eyes, I could tell that the SPLA was more potent. They had clothes that blended into the trees, and all the SPLA had guns. People started to wonder out loud if perhaps this SPLA could stop the northerners.

The SPLA was not strong enough to beat the northern army. Not yet, anyway. They were being equipped, funded and supported by Ethiopia but they lacked the manpower to conduct effective offensives. Their thin ranks were being decimated by the airpower of the north, and often cut down by the inter-tribal conflict. Many SPLA recruits had even been killed by the Anyanya as they tried to make it to the rebel bases across the border in Ethiopia, before the amalgamation of the groups happened.

The SPLA needed manpower, and they were going to get it from the only abundant source left in the country: the rural villages that were now populated mostly by women, the elderly and children.

It would be unthinkable to bring women into the war, and the elderly would not even last the journey to the SPLA bases, but the boy children could pull the trigger of an AK-47 almost as well as their uncles and fathers. They could be groomed for extreme loyalty also, and they would not baulk at some of the aspects of fighting that some men could not stomach.

The fighting of this war was not only done on the battle-field, and those who needed to be killed were not only just men carrying guns.

The SPLA would build an army of war boys. I would be a part of that army. I would be a war boy.

I remember how I spent my last day as a civilian – I played at being a man. I sat with our tame cow, which didn't go out to graze in the fields but stayed close to home to give milk. I pretended to own her, and gave her stern orders, which she acknowledged only with blank stares and defecation. My voice changed when I told her that one day I would probably have to give her over to another man, another man with a very fine daughter who would be strong enough to carry an antelope on each shoulder, and who would be so tall that she could touch the roof of a cattle shed just by reaching up.

I rubbed the cow's neck apologetically. There were more blank stares and more dropped shit.

In the dirt at the cow's feet, I designed my own cattle camp. This was one of my favourite games – moulding clumps of wet dirt representing all the cows I hoped to own, penned in by a dirt fence, with twigs and sticks for the trees my cows would need for shade and a ditch dug with my heel representing the Nile.

When my camp was finished, I would move the mud cows around and imagine all the sons that would be working for me. I'd also compose the songs that would be written about my life – songs of hunting and fishing, wrestling and cow herding, songs about tall wives, and strong sons.

There would be no songs for me, however, because that would be the last day I would spend in my village as a villager.

That was the day that I fell off the edge of the world of children, and landed in another world. I did not land in the world of men though – the world I yearned to be a part of – but another world. In this world there was no family, and no gods, no Nile eagles and no *Nhialic*. In this new world there was only one thing: the machine that is war.

I was destined to be a useful part of that machine, or I was destined to be dead. I was no longer Little Swallow, or the God Eater, and not even Deng Adut. I was SPLA. I would be that or I would be nothing.

On that day I was seven years old.

Chapter Two

THE RIBBON OF BOYS

There had been fierce fighting the few days before I was taken. The northern men had driven past the track next to the Nile in the morning, and when they returned in the afternoon, they had been attacked. After the battle, the SPLA came to the village – as they often did – to get food, goats and rest, but they were also coming to the chief with an edict from their leader, Kuol Manyang Juuk, to gather at least one boy-child from each family.

The chief had no choice but to acquiesce – our village was in SPLA territory now, and SPLA territory was under gun rule.

The word went down to the clans, and then to the mothers. Athieu Akau Deng was told that she must give me up to the army. I don't know what the feeling may have been in her heart when she heard, but I know inside she would have been collapsing. It is a pragmatic life, however, Sudanese village life, so knowing that there was no refusing the order, my mother of mothers started to prepare food for my trip.

Adut the stammerer was sent out to tell me to prepare for a long journey.

I don't remember how I learned that Adut was coming for me with bad news, but I knew because I ran from him and hid in a tall tree with a great many leaves. I did not want to go on a journey, especially a long journey.

Adut and some of the other men searched through the afternoon and the night, but they couldn't find me. I came down from that tree at dawn as I thought the danger had passed. Adut must have found some other boy to be sent off into the world.

He hadn't though and he caught up with me in the morning, while I was playing with my little make-believe cattle camp. He approached me as one might a dog with pinned-back ears – walking slowly, leading with a gift of cloth in his hand. It was the gift that kept me from running away.

Adut told me that I had been selected to be educated. He told me I must go away from my mother for a while. He told me I would come back. He told me I had to be strong and that I would be going to Ethiopia. I didn't know what Ethiopia was, but I knew my mother wouldn't be there and I didn't want to leave her.

The gift in Adut's hand was an army-issue khaki shirt. I cried as he placed it around my shoulders.

'T-t-t-take this sh-sh-sh-shirt, and may you wear it p-p-p-proudly on the journey,' Adut said.

'Do you kn-kn-kn-know proudly?'

I did.

I had never worn any clothes before, let alone a fine khaki shirt like that. I left the shirt on my shoulders because I knew that I would be going to this Ethiopia, no matter what my wishes were. There was no point in refusing the gift. I was curious about being educated. I knew it was a great thing to be educated, but I hoped it didn't take very long.

As we prepared to leave the village, I found that I was not the only boy from my *luak* who had been selected to go away. My cousins Anyang Aluel, Adut Agor and Kueric Thuch – also tiny, crying and shivering with fear – would be travelling to Ethiopia too.

As the men waited, my mother held me one last time. She held me too long though, and her fear started to seep into me. I began to cry so she broke the embrace. The last touch I felt was her hand on mine as she gave me a parcel of sorghum, grain and nuts.

'You will have to be strong now, Little Swallow. You can no longer afford to be soft.'

There were thirty boys selected from my village – some a little older than me, some younger – and we were all marched, in one column, into the bush by some village elders. After a couple of hours of marching, I was as far from my birthplace as I'd ever been.

It was roughly twenty kilometres to Kolnyang, the first town we stopped in. I thought the journey was hard. I thought that my feet hurt, my stomach was empty, and my mouth was dry. I had no idea.

When we got to Kolnyang I saw two things my young eyes had never seen before. The first was a structure with a large tin roof, which made me wonder if Kolnyang was one of those things called a city that some of the Anyanya had spoken of. The second was the great expanse of people.

These people were spread far further than the limits of the town and my eyes. Most of the people were boys – their eyes full of suspicion and fear, and tears, sitting or lying on the baked dirt – but there were also soldiers, who smoked, and looked bored and tired and annoyed, as only soldiers can.

In Kolnyang most of the boys and men were Dinka – although not all were Dinka-Bor – but some were from different tribes. I could tell that by their faces, and their bodies, and the language they used. Due to this mix of tribes, I was more fearful of this town than the bush and its hungry animals. In my village, I rarely met anyone from another tribe.

We stayed overnight in Kolnyang, bivouacking with everyone else, but at the setting of the sun, no children's songs were sung. The only sound in the camp was a muted whimpering.

I did not sleep, and I don't think anyone else did either, except of course the soldiers.

The crying got quieter as the moon rose, but the sound of the boys never totally went away. When I sat up in the middle of the night I saw that almost every pair of eyes around me were open. I knew what all the eyes were looking at. They were looking at the stars. The mothers would not be sleeping that night, either. The stars were perhaps the last thing that could be shared by both the mothers and the boys.

I knew that my mother would be looking at those stars that night.

At dawn the journey started in earnest. Our group would not start to walk until the sun was high in the sky however, as a great number of clans were sent on the path before us. When we joined the march, there was a ribbon of boys and soldiers in front of us that stretched all the way to the horizon. After a few hours of walking, the ribbon stretched out behind us, too.

The first day in the ribbon of boys was the easiest. There was still food and water, and there were trees for shade sometimes, and the blisters on my feet were not yet leaking blood. The soldiers had not yet become desperate and angry, and, in some of us, there was even a sense of awe at being part of something as massive as this horizon-spanning column. Any awe died on the third day.

One boy complained constantly on the trip. He was perhaps slightly older than me, and as we marched he was given the name Adhal Ayor, which means 'a child who is disrespectful of the elders'.

After every couple of hours of walking, Adhal Ayor would sit on the grass, only moving on when prompted by a soldier.

'If you fall behind, you will be left for the animals to fill their stomachs,' one of the SPLA soldiers told him.

We heard the sounds of lions as we walked, and I think the growls helped Adhal Ayor to find the strength to keep walking. I don't know whether Adhal Ayor made it all the way to Ethiopia, but I think it's likely he did not.

On the second day we walked from Kolnyang to a Dinka-Bor village called Ajageer, and on the third day we pressed on into Murle lands.

We knew the moment we crossed into Murle territory because whispers started to ripple up and down the line. A new level of fear started to spread – the fear of being taken. The Murle were a tribe of expert guerilla fighters and often raided our lands to steal those things that were most sacred to us – cattle, children and our mothers. Being in the ribbon of boys was bad, but at least there were cousins and uncles around us. We were not in our villages, but – for the time being – we had food and water. Who knew what happened to the boys who were stolen by the Murle?

For most of the boys their fear of the Murle had existed almost since birth. My fear of the Murle coalesced around a gunshot wound that one of my mothers had on her shoulder when she had been shot in one of the Murle's many raids.

The soldiers were constantly on edge as we walked. They kept their rifles at the ready, and their eyes on the bush. Sometimes shots would echo from behind or ahead of us. Sometimes a ripple of chatter would come all the way to us, explaining the shots. Usually it was some soldiers hunting antelope, but sometimes it was not.

When the Murle attacked us, they came in groups of three or four. Knowing that a frontal attack was impossible, they shot their precious bullets only when they knew they would find a target and then they would disappear again, like ghosts. There were many Murle attacks.

I don't know if the Murle stole any of the boys on that journey, but I know some were killed. Soldiers were killed too. Bodies large and small were left to the animals because the column never slowed, such was the inertia of the ribbon.

That night we stopped at a Murle town called Gummero that had been occupied by a garrison of SPLA fighters. We stopped for just a few hours – the last proper night's sleep was behind us – and no one managed to get any sleep in that town. The stories of kidnap and death were too powerful a stimulant, regardless of how tired we all were.

The next day, like zombies, we once again crossed into wild Murle lands, and the next day after that. There were more shots, and more stories and more bodies. When we would stop at the end of each day I would experience moments of unconsciousness, but I'm not sure I ever achieved something that I previously would have called sleep.

After leaving Gummero we crossed a desert, which was something I'd not conceived of let alone seen. I knew that the sky could be empty, but the land also? The land was full of trees, and rivers, and animals and people, as far as I knew, but it seemed there could be emptiness below the horizon also.

After a few hours in the desert there was only dirt and sand as far as the eye could see in any direction. One of my great-uncles – Garang Kudhur, an experienced soldier from the Anyanya – told us that from that point on the only liquid that went anywhere was in a mouth, until we could see a body of drinking water in front of us. No matter what we heard from the line in front of us, or even if we saw a town, we must see this water with our own eyes before we could wash, or cool down with water.

We trudged and trudged and trudged and for hours we could see only desert and could hear only the sound of our feet, except for the occasional howl or wail from an animal. We received water only a couple of times a day, and then it was just a slug from a jerry can. Soon the jerry cans started to run dry and our ration became a shot from the cap. After that we were only given enough water to wet our tongues – just enough to stop your mouth from cracking and bleeding.

After a few days in the desert some of the older boys started to act in a way that would have normally been seen as madness. Some ate mud when they found it, and others fought to drink the urine that was expelled when another soldier or a boy (apparently a soldier or boy with a far greater water reserve than us – we never urinated in the desert) stopped to take a leak.

The trek went on, everlasting. I lost any sense of time or place and I even started to lose the idea that there would be an end to the march. The thirst, the sun boring into me, and the pain in my stomach and feet was the only reality I understood. The fatigue was as infinite as the view in front of me. The walk could not get any worse, and it would surely not get any better. It just was, and would forever be.

The monotony was finally broken when I collapsed on the path that had been trodden by the thousands of boys in front of me. I did not try to collapse, nor did I try not to, it's just what happened.

I lay there on the dirt as blistered feet trudged past my face. I was not the first boy who had fallen with fatigue, and in each instance the soldiers had done a quick triage assessment. Could the boy be compelled to stand and go on? Could the boy be carried until he recharged his ability to walk on unassisted? If the answer to both questions was 'no', then the boy's fate was left to the compassion of the boys and soldiers behind him, and compassion was necessarily in short supply.

Most boys were being marched by members of their clan or family members. If their clan or family had decided that they were too far gone to be helped, then they were almost certainly not going to be picked up by strangers.

A feast was being left for the beasts of the desert, but I was not to be a course. I was picked up and carried by one of my group – I do not know who. I was bouncing in and out of consciousness. We must have stopped to rest when I was unconscious, because I remember waking as everyone lay on the ground quiet, and I remember waking again as the others were preparing to move on.

I managed to walk on. I went back to the groove of endless sun and pain.

I don't know if it was something that had always been planned, or if it was because too many boys were being left behind, but at some point in the desert march, a water truck was sent along the line. Jerry cans were filled, but they soon became empty again.

I started to think that there might be an end to the trip when I saw a huge shimmering expanse of water ahead on the horizon. For hours we marched towards it, but it seemed no matter how many steps we put under us, we weren't getting any closer to the water.

It was an effort to speak, but I asked one of the soldiers how far he thought we were to that water. It was the only question that was answered on that journey.

'Not water. It's a trick of the eyes,' he croaked.

I cursed my eyes. There was no water in front of us, but mercifully, after a few more hours, there was a border nearby, which was delineated by a change of terrain.

When we finally crossed into Ethiopia, there were green trees, and animals and grass and a wide, and very welcome river. I now know that that river was never far from where we were forced to march. There were boys who were left behind for the animals unnecessarily. I do not know why.

Our first stop in Ethiopia was in a border town called Pachella – a beautiful settlement on the banks of the Blue Nile, which we couldn't enjoy at all. We were as fearful in Pachella as we had been in the Murle towns, because in Pachella we saw men with light skin, and the only light-skinned men we'd seen before had come to our villages to kill.

In Pachella, we were given our first military rations. Soldiers with giant bags of corn came around each camp, handing out food for the boys. For us boys, they counted out the individual kernels of corn as they put them in our hands.

We stayed in Pachella for some days. Ethiopian soldiers and the SPLA had occupied the town, but they had no control of the road ahead. There were Murle on the road, as well as Anuak, the people of the lands we were in, both of which had been known to attack SPLA patrols to steal their guns and ammunition.

There was also the threat of northern planes and helicopters. If spies told the northerners about a cluster of boys and soldiers on that road, a great haul of bodies could be attained with just a few bombs.

Eventually we were moved onto the road, and it was a long one. We were given small amounts of corn and water along the way, but we were not going to make it unless we augmented what we were provided. Some Anuak tribesmen traded food – a grain-mash that was a by-product of their beer – on the line, and we bought it with what we had: the khaki shirt that my brother had given to me when we started the journey.

I was once again naked, but now many hundreds of miles from my village.

Eventually we stopped at a wooded area close to a river. This was Pinyudo, a camp that we boys would help build, and a place that a generation of southern Sudanese boys would either pass through, or die in.

For the rest of the world, Pinyudo was (and still is) a refugee camp, but for those of us there at its inception, the camp was a holding pen for boys, a place of incubation and maturation. It was a place where the SPLA could store their human stock until we became large enough to be able to accept the recoil of an assault rifle, and plunge a bayonet into a foe.

The first few months in Pinyudo were dedicated to building grass tents, cutting bush, clearing paths and roads. My sole role in life then was hauling water from the river to the camp. It was months of monotony. My feet flattened a path from the camp to the river, and the jerry cans carved an odd-looking bald spot on the top of my head where they spent most of the journey from the river back to the camp.

Those were empty days. There was no play, no fun, no movement, no purpose, and certainly no songs. All I did was try to keep up with the water deliveries, and get some food in my belly when I could. Some days I did not manage it, as the food was often stolen by the older boys.

I left my village fat and with khaki around my shoulders. After just a few weeks in Pinyudo, I was naked, tiny and quite fragile.

Sicknesses like measles, tuberculosis, whooping cough and chickenpox swept through the camp in waves. Eventually one of these fever-inducing diseases cut me down.

My journeys from the river became slower and slower, and soon I couldn't eat and could only barely drink. My skin got hotter and hotter and eventually I couldn't get up and leave my tent. In keeping with the conventional bush remedy for fever, I was placed in a corn sack and left outside in the sun.

The days went by and I only got sicker and more feverish until one of the soldiers dragged me to one of the larger grass huts, which served as a field hospital. There were dozens of boys in sacks in that 'hospital', including my cousin Anyang Aluel, who was taken from my *luak* with me.

We would look at each other, when we had the strength, and nod an acknowledgement across the hut. Anyang had gone through a transformation also. His belly had shrunk, and his cheeks had become shallow, and most of the time his eyes stared straight ahead as though he was thinking about something very large.

Yar Deng, one of the few women in the camp, and a relative of mine, treated my cousin and I with small portions of porridge, and large needles. The needles I reeled from and the porridge I routinely vomited up.

Every day some of the boys in the hut died. When they did, thread and needles were produced, and the opening of their corn sack was sewn closed. These sacks were placed in a large hole nearby.

Perhaps thirty or forty boys were taken to the hut after that particular outbreak. As far as I could tell, only two regained health. I was one of them. Anyang Aluel was not.

As they sewed up the top of his sack, I started to conceive of what it meant to be put in the hole. I was only seven and had not previously understood that the people who were cut down by the bombs, the boys who were left in the desert, my father under his mound next to the *luak*, and the sucked-away cousin disappearing from view next to me were never, ever coming back to life.

The finality of death only occurred to me then. Death had been around me for months, but I had never really understood it until Anyang Aluel, whose life circumstances had been almost exactly the same as mine, was dumped into a hole full of boys. I knew then that death was forever.

While I was recovering from my sickness, all of the boys were called to parade. Parades were not an unusual occurrence. We were often barked into formation, and then screamed at in Arabic for an hour or two by an officer, before having someone explain to us what the yelling was all about. This parade, however, would not be like the others.

From the time we got to Pinyudo, almost all of us boys had been overseen by soldiers and older boys, or even extended family, from our own clan. The sub-camps that had been established were largely homogenous, with all of the boys with me being Dinka-Bor and speaking the same language.

Now, however, this parade was ordering everyone be mixed up. After the parade – we were told – no two boys from one clan should put their shoulders together. This was the rule, and breaking the rule would elicit a harsh punishment.

I suspect the reason for this move was to kill fomenting dissent. Disease and malnutrition were killing many of the younger and weaker boys, and the older boys and soldiers mourned their brothers and cousins, and perhaps also saw a future where their strength might fail them too.

After the mixing parade, my brother John, who had been ordered to the camp from the front lines, sought me out. John and I had not seen each other since I had been taken from our village, and I was surprised that he recognised me – small, sick and shivering as I was.

At seventeen John was a veteran then, even though he would barely be considered a man anywhere else in the world. He had been fighting in the war for some years, and had more than once been left for dead after being seriously injured with bullets and artillery.

I was happy to see him. John had always been an incandescent presence, and in him I saw a larger world than the small, awful world I was living in. Brothers were not supposed to be brothers that day though, and John and I only had a few moments together before he was barked away by another SPLA officer. In the time that we did have together, John took off his shirt – which was cotton, red and beautiful – and put it on me.

'Things are hard, Little Swallow, but you will survive in this shirt,' he said. 'It will protect you from being sick, and from being hungry.'

I knew that John had special Christian magic, so I held that shirt reverently. This protective shirt was the second piece of clothing I'd ever worn. Perhaps it worked too because when I wore the shirt I was neither sick nor hungry. I only wore it for a few minutes, however. As I was walking over to report at my new camp, a fist crashed into the back of my head, and then some feet into my stomach. I was robbed of my only possession, and walked to my new home naked.

I was shivering, mute and feeling the blows when I reported to an older boy of perhaps thirteen or fourteen, named James Mading Mabil. As was the case with many of the teenagers who were in command of a group of younger boys, the lesser angels of James Mading Mabil often ruled his moods, and he was sometimes prone to cruelty.

Nearly every day after that mixing parade, I woke up soaked in my own urine. When James Mading Mabil found me sticky or smelling foul, he wouldn't beat me – he would order the police to do it. There were boy police just like there were boy soldiers.

For many months after the mixing parade, I spoke to no one except for a grunt or a nod. I was sick and hungry every day, and my only activity was hauling jerry cans of water from the river to the camp – an activity that would soon strike me mute with fear as I knew that dropping the water would mean a beating from James Mading Mabil.

Of course I went mad.

It happened one day when we were called to parade. Once we were settled and at attention, a great number of soldiers – far more than I'd ever seen at parade before – walked in, with most fanned around one man who was obviously more important than all of the others put together.

The man wore a military uniform and cap, and he had eyes that were set close together, which made him look very thoughtful, and a wide mouth that was framed by a well-kept chin-strap beard. This man was Dr John Garang, the leader of the SPLA, and the father of South Sudanese independence.

When Dr Garang was seated some of the older and fatter soldiers took turns giving speeches. When there were pauses in the speeches we would all clap and cheer enthusiastically, even though many of us didn't know what was being said. Some of the older soldiers led us in war songs, most of which I knew. I sang them as loudly as I could, as I knew James Mading Mabil would be watching.

Then, flanked by some fat SPLA soldiers whose uniforms I didn't recognise, some near-naked men were marched, blindfolded and bound, in front of us. As I was sitting at the very front of the parade, I could see the trembling fingers of the blindfolded men and the patches of urine collecting around their private parts.

One of the commanders spoke angrily and forcefully to us and the blindfolded men. Then the commander motioned to the fat soldiers. They walked a few paces from their prisoners, raised their rifles and, at the commander's mark, fired into the heads and bodies of the blindfolded men.

Brain and bone and blood splayed out on the ground and sky and over the front row of boys. The human matter that landed on me did not affect me that much, nor did the rolling *crack* of the shots, or the way the men fell and twitched spasmodically. The smell was too much, though.

There was a smell that escaped the bodies after each shot that lingered in my nose. It smelled like fresh rot, if there could be such a thing. It was familiar, but also strange and terrifying.

My legs moved without any order. They were not taking me anywhere specific, but away from that smell of living death. My feet slapped on the ground and I heard the heaving of my breath. I heard shouting behind me. Another boy, perhaps a year or two older than me, ran past in a panic, and then another. They had responded as I had. The last boy was wearing shoes made out of old truck tyre rubber and nails, one of which he lost while running.

I barely felt the pain as the nail of his shoe entered the arch of my foot. Blood poured on the ground below and the dirt stuck to my foot.

I was limping by the time I was caught by James Mading Mabil. I expected to be beaten, but in that wretched moment Mabil's better angels took over. He took me back to the camp and treated my foot. The wound did not get any better, though.

Each day I would examine the hole in my foot, looking for signs of healing, and every day I would find as much dirt and blood and pus as I'd found the day before. Then one day I found movement in the hole. Bugs called 'jiggers' – small, crawling animals like slimy, legless ants – had taken up in my wound. I dug the jiggers out of my foot, but they had laid eggs, so there were always more whenever I looked.

Fever soon returned to my blood, and, with the pain in my foot, and the smell of the executed men confusing me, my thoughts soon could not be lined up properly. I started to lose my memory of words. I started to have trouble remembering the route to the river, despite it being almost a straight line, and I forgot which bed was mine. For a time, I did not understand the correlation between the wetness I would wake up in each morning and the slaps and kicks I would receive during the day. I could not remember what was food and what wasn't.

There was more than one occasion when I was eating what I thought was food but it was actually human excrement that I had picked up from the ground.

I fought hard to keep the memory of my mother in my mind, though. She was my last link to my old life. All of the energy that was left in me was used remembering her name, and what her eyes looked like before I walked away from my village.

After a few weeks of fever, reality had almost completely escaped me. Most days when I woke, there was a haze on the plain just past the camp and I could not escape the idea that it was the smoke of my uncle Gongich Ngueny Deng's cattle camp. When I saw that haze, I could taste the fresh milk he would be filling in skins, and the recently caught fish that he would be roasting.

I thought I could eat and drink and get fat, like I had been, if I could just manage to get to that camp. Perhaps I could take milk to my mother, and with her guidance, I could get older. If only I could get to the smoke of Uncle Gongich's fire, I could perhaps have my own cattle camp.

I would run, limping but with gusto, for the haze, only to be dragged back by one of the older boys. Back at the tents, I would be beaten and admonished. When the haze had dissipated, I would go about my water-bringing day, but the next morning, with the haze back, the mad routine would happen all over again.

Soon, to keep me from running away in the morning, I was tied to the bed each evening, and only released when the sun was high in the sky.

Eventually my foot got better, but not my mind, nor my blood. In the mornings I would strain against the ropes until, as the fever rose and rose, I had no straining left in me. Eventually, I could not stand when ordered.

In those weeks I would have wasted to nothing except that my cousin Adut Agor took it upon himself to feed and bathe me. He had also seen Anyang waste away to death, and he could not bear to see it happen again to his kin.

Adut would carry me around the camp on his back, and he was usually kind and compassionate to me, except that he complained about my jutting bones stabbing him in the back. He would take me to the hospital and try to get the nurses to fix me. Sometimes I would be allowed to lie down on one of the cot beds for a while, but they could never fix me.

I was Adut's burden for weeks and weeks. I shed even more weight, and my bones become as sharp as knives. My fever burned, I soiled myself whenever I managed to eat and drink, and I made no sense when I spoke. Yet Adut bore it all until, one day, while I was lying on a cot in the hospital, he said he had reached the end of his tether.

'Deng, I am not strong. Your bones stab me when I carry you, and my muscles ache at the end of the day. I have sores and sickness and we cannot go on. I think you are on the way into the ground. Perhaps you should just make it easier for both of us.'

I knew he was right.

'We are all dead soon anyway, so we shouldn't suffer too much.'

My mind was everywhere, except where sense lived, but in that moment I understood what my cousin was telling me. I had a moment of clarity. I must die now. He must be free of me.

Considering how frail my mind and body were, I thought that I would be able to die by rolling off the camp cot. I tried to do just that, but I did not have the strength to get off the edge.

'You must help me,' I said to Adut.

He couldn't. Adut left me. I hoped he was coming back with a gun so I could die like the blindfolded men. For a

46

moment I thought about the dead–alive smell I hated so much, but after a while I felt better when I realised that I would not have to suffer that smell, and that, for Adut, that smell would be preferable to having to carry my sharp bones around the camp until it was time for him to die.

I waited for Adut and the gun. I waited and waited and waited, and night fell and day came, and night fell again, but Adut never came. I would have to stay alive. I would have to be a soldier and fight in the war.

I was nine years old.

Chapter Three

THE LAND OF WAR

When I was nine I knew nothing of the war, or of the history of my nation. I only knew the lore of the Dinka. I knew that the Dinka world started when, one day, men emerged from the Nile with cows following them, as there is no world without milk, meat and dowry.

I knew that those early men used to go back to heaven via a long rope after they died, so *Nhialic* could fix their broken bodies and then send them back to their fields.

I knew that the rope was now gone, because a woman walked out of the Nile. One day when this woman was pounding grain, a baby bluebird tried to eat the grain. The woman killed the baby bluebird and the mother bluebird, seeing her dead chick, chewed through the rope to heaven, and in that moment, man became mortal.

That was the history that I knew, but it did not explain the war that I was thrust into. In fact, very few Dinka people believed that our history could explain this new war as it dragged on, so people started to renounce the traditional history and align themselves with John's god.

To understand the myriad motivations of the people involved in this new war, you needed an adult's perspective.

Before Sudan was a country, it was an Arabic saying and a loose geographical designation. *Bilad as-sudan* translates literally into 'land of the blacks', and is what conquering Arab military commanders called the area in Africa that sits just below the Saharan Desert.

Bilad as-sudan was home to many African kingdoms over many centuries, but during the rise of the Ottoman Empire at around the fifteenth century, Islamic rule was slowly established in the north of what is now the nation of Sudan. By the mid nineteenth century, Sudan's capital Khartoum and its surrounding satellite cities were a mix of Nubian and Arabic cultures, but the south of the country, a fierce and underdeveloped area that is now the nation of South Sudan, remained largely immune to Arabisation and to Islam.

The north flourished in the Ottoman period until, in the late nineteenth century, harsh taxation policies and pressure from Europe to limit the lucrative slave trade fomented dissent, which coalesced around a Messianic Islamic warrior priest named Muhammad Ahmad.

Using the fuel of powerful religious and nationalistic rhetoric, Ahmad built up a large flock of acolyte-militiamen and, in 1881, proclaimed himself to be a Mahdi (a guided or enlightened one) and the true leader of the area known as Sudan.

The governance of the Mahdists was defined by brutal proselytising and conquering. Beaten foes could either submit to the strictest interpretation of sharia law, or be put to death as apostates. For the length of the Mahdi's reign, that dichotomy of religion or death continued.

Once the Mahdi rebellion had successfully taken Khartoum, the Mahdi changed his title to *Khalifa*, which literally translates as successor or steward but also denotes a leader that rules with the approval of God.

The Mahdists proved a particularly efficient fighting force but, like most forces entering South Sudan, they won battles but didn't manage to influence or control the people. Still, their brutality spread and spread, even outside the nation's borders, with campaigns extending deep into Eritrea and Ethiopia.

Eventually, European forces defeated the Mahdi in the late 1890s. The great governments of the time were not particularly concerned with the fates of most of the east African colonies, but when a Mahdist army pushed deep into the continent-straddling nation of Egypt, a counter-offensive was ordered.

Historically, the story of the defeat of the Mahdi has been subsumed by the enormity of World War I, but it should be noted that nearly one thousand New South Welshmen were committed to the defeat of the Mahdists as part of a British force. Eventually the caliphate was toppled by a campaign headed by legendary British commander Lord H.H. Kitchener.

As a result, for the first half of the twentieth century the British – either directly or by proxy – ruled what is modern Sudan and South Sudan. For that period the nation was largely at peace, thanks in no small part to British recognition that Sudan was not one country, but at least two, with the north being predominantly culturally Arabic and religiously Islamic, and the south being tribal, traditional and either Christian or animist.

Those two Sudans were ruled largely independently until, in 1946, the British decided that the two administrative regions should be merged. Following World War II, the tensions between Sudan's north and south grew. While

Britain's power and interest waned in the country, the north gained more and more power over the south, and they lost representation, consideration and the benefits of taxation. Eventually things came to a head when, in 1955, the British prepared to give complete autonomy to a government which was increasingly being constituted by, and for, Arabs, Muslims and northerners.

On 1 January 1956 Sudan gained independence, and the new government instantly inherited a guerilla war that had started a few months earlier when a series of army bases in the south conducted mutinies.

For the first few years of what would eventually be called the First Sudanese Civil War, the southern fighters were largely disorganised and ineffective, thanks in no small part to the internal tribal distrust and infighting that still to this day plagues the nation of South Sudan.

The southern rebellion was helped by the fact that the new Sudanese government, mostly consisting of northerners and Muslims, was also suffering crippling disharmony. The ineffectual war continued for some time until a Madi leader took command of the disparate groups of southern fighters and, for the most part, put them under a central command.

When that happened, the fighting was given another name, and that name was the Anyanya Rebellion.

After proving to be somewhat effective against the government forces, the Anyanya gained financial and material support from the enemies of Khartoum, including Sudan's largely Christian neighbour Ethiopia.

The Anyanya Rebellion lasted many years, and caused the deaths of hundreds of thousands of people from the south.

The rebellion ended in 1972 when some very large Christian and Islamic groups brought the government and the Anyanya to a peace conference in Ethiopia's capital, Addis Ababa. The main concession offered to the south was that the southern part of the nation would be governed as one administrative district, with certain limited powers of self-determination.

When the peace agreement was signed, many former Anyanya field commanders voiced their concerns that the concessions agreed upon were too weak for the peace to be maintained. Those commanders said that nothing short of independence would suffice to guarantee peace, and many maintained their forces, ready to commence fighting if need be.

An imperfect peace lasted until the early 1980s, when a block of Islamists gained political power in the capital and insisted that Sudan should be a wholly Islamic nation. The group ordained that the south should live under sharia law, with stoning and amputations legal punishments for transgressions such as apostasy.

Khartoum dismantled the special autonomy laws that had been agreed upon after the Addis Ababa accords and seized the oilfields in the south that had been generating the bulk of the revenue bankrolling the south's limited independence.

The disgruntled Anyanya commanders reactivated their forces and dissent even fomented within the northern Sudanese army.

One southern colonel, who'd been absorbed into Khartoum's army after the end of the Anyanya Rebellion planned a mutiny. That officer's name was Dr John Garang.

In 1983 Dr Garang – who was ethnically Dinka – had been sent by Khartoum to Bor, a Dinka town, to pacify a southern garrison on the verge of revolt. Instead, he killed the northern soldiers in the town and took the southern soldiers into the bush. There they were re-formed as an anti-government force named the Sudanese People's Liberation Army, the SPLA.

With help from neighbouring Christian nations, the SPLA become an effective force. Khartoum was forced to the negotiating table, but this time the SPLA would accept nothing less than independence. In 1991 negotiations completely fell apart. Both sides prepared for war.

The north prepared itself for a short, modern war, buying up fighter jets, bombers and helicopters. The south prepared itself for a long, guerilla war, enacting general conscription, and then scooping up boys like me from the southern villages like mine, so they could be deployed against the northern soldiers.

It was a long and brutal war. When the fighting finally ceased the butcher's bill was estimated to be roughly two million dead, with most of those dying of starvation, drought or disease.

There would have been short odds on me being counted in that number of dead, but I did not die, in one instance because of men in blue hats. Men in blue hats, and wheat that they brought from a country a long way away that is called 'Australia'.

Chapter Four

A KILLER IS BORN

Before I could find a way to die, the camp at Pinyudo transformed around me. Women were brought to the camp, and girls and *kawaja*, which is what we Dinka call white men. I had never seen any white men before. At first I was confused because I assumed they were Arabs, then I thought they were those lighter-skinned men from the SPLA that I had seen at the border, but they didn't act like either of those groups of men, and, besides, they were so white they were actually pink.

These white men wore blue hats and brought food and medicine. They fixed my fever and soon I could walk, carry water and think a thought that coincided with reality.

There were all kinds of new food in the camp when the blue-hatted *kawaja* came, with the best being a type of wheat that we called *digigstralia*. We would mix that *digigstralia* with oil, and cook it on hot metal plates. Even now, the thought makes my mouth water.

Digigstralia was the most coveted of all the food that the white men brought. When we saw boxes of it – which we could identify by a blue rectangle with white stars and red lines in the top left-hand corner – we would practically vibrate with happiness.

Digigstralia was a combination of the word *digig* – a local term for flour – and our best attempt at saying the word 'Australia', which was where the blue-hatted men said the food came from.

The blue-hatted men issued me clothes – a pair of white shorts and a singlet. I wore that outfit proudly for at least a year. When there were holes in my shorts I'd spend days hunting for scraps of cloth so I could patch up the gaps. When there were lice in my clothes, I'd spend hours baking them on the banks of the river in the searing sands to kill the parasites and their eggs.

I was proud of how I looked in my clothes, but they also had a functional purpose as, when stuffed with cardboard, they acted like armour against the beatings with sticks that I still suffered from the older boys from time to time.

This protection was especially necessary when a disease that I am yet to identify – manifested by weeping, welting rashes on the buttocks – swept through the camp. Arses were sore all across the camp, and I remember one of the boys, who had been washing in the river, ran screaming as fish began eating the exposed strips of his buttock flesh.

Things were still difficult then, but life was also easier than it had been before. Boys were still dying, but at a lesser rate. It was good to wear clothes and eat food. I started to remember who I was, and where I was from, and I started to remember that there had been people who had cared about me.

We started worshipping those *kawaja* because they usually brought food, clothes, utensils or medicine with them when they came. The other boys and I would compose light-hearted children's songs – the first any of us had sung since we'd been in our villages – about these magic people of abundance, and we'd sing them heartily when the white men came into the camp.

The SPLA were also happy when the *kawaja* came into the camp, but only if the soldiers had been tipped off before they came. Before the white men arrived, the soldiers had much to do: their uniforms had to be changed, their guns stowed, and the wooden training guns taken from the older boys.

I think that the SPLA accepted, and probably even facilitated the UN ostensibly taking control of the camp. The SPLA was losing a lot of human cargo in that fetid holding pen. With help from the blue-hatted men of the UN, the SPLA would lose fewer boys, and have far stronger boys when it came time for them to start their military training in earnest.

My military training really started when I was nine. One day when the *kawaja* were far from the camp, a group of boys my age were called to parade and there our heights were measured against an upright AK-47. Those like me who were taller than the gun were told that we were moving on from the camp.

I had been close to dying before the camp improved, so I was wary of a new change of circumstances. But I also couldn't help but feel some excitement at what felt like a progression. Ironically, I had started to feel more like a soldier since the *kawaja* had come. The white men were outsiders – welcome outsiders, but outsiders nonetheless – and their world of food and clothes seemed less real than the world of parade, training with wooden guns (which I had started to do when they came), and hearing about the glorious victories on the front line.

Camp life had seemed disorganised and random, but it had been effective because at the time when the SPLA needed me to start thinking like a soldier, I was doing just that. I enjoyed having a wooden gun in my hands, and I no longer hated parade. The discipline that had seemed so brutal started to feel second nature to me. In fact, it started to feel necessary.

In the weeks before we were taken to our second camp I had started to think about the northern men who had come to our village. I now knew what death was, and I was starting to think about what it would be like to deal it out.

It was a two-hour march through the bush to our new camp, which was very different from the old one. When we had walked into Pinyudo, there was nothing but bush, and even when we left there was little more than canvas tents, some wells and tracks and roads. When I arrived at the new camp, I marched into a military installation, with gates, ammunition dumps, machine-gun nests, barracks and firing ranges.

From the moment I stepped over the border of that camp I was very much an SPLA soldier.

We were taken to a barrack and placed under the command of a squad leader, which was usually an older boy who could read or write. Each squad, which constituted ten boys, was assigned two other sister squads, which made up a platoon. The platoons also picked up four other platoons to make a brigade.

From the moment we walked through the gate, it was drilled into us that our squad mates, our platoon mates and our brigade mates were now the most important people in our lives. My brigade was my new tribe, the boys of my platoon were my extended family, and my squad mates were my new brothers.

There were replacements for my mother and father too, which were my AK-47 and Dr John Garang. Nothing was more important to me in my life than my rifle and my leader – that was drilled into me every day of my training. For months I trained with a wooden gun, but I dreamed of the day when I would have my own rifle, with the power to fight and kill, and fulfil my purpose designed by my leader.

Without the direction of Dr John Garang I was listless, and without my weapon I was ineffective. With one in my heart and the other in my hands, there was no limit to what I could do.

My unit was called the *kamanch* (claw hammer) brigade, under commanding officer, Paul Ring Dau. Dau was my link to the wisdom of Dr John Garang, which would filter down via the brigade leader, then the platoon leader and finally my squad leader.

The discipline in that military camp was extreme and violent, but it worked because our leaders had started to establish purpose, and it seemed that almost every boy bought in. For those who didn't, they would most likely not survive. Executions were a regular occurrence. Every day in that camp, the war seemed to come closer to us, and in war, you fight and take orders or you die.

In that camp we slowly but surely became effective, faithful killers.

One day we were called to parade, and a group of older boys marched in front of us before being deployed to the front lines. To see them, firm and stoic, with their weapons that they would soon use, marching in front of us made us burn with jealousy. Being issued an AK-47, and then sent off to a place where there was an endless supply of northern men to kill was what every boy in the camp wanted. My only consolation was that I knew one day I would be joining them in glorious battle.

We would have to wait much longer than any of us expected, though.

Unbeknownst to us boys, there was another war raging nearby, and that war was to spin us young recruits off the axis of combat that the SPLA had planned for us.

It happened one evening, when we were confined to barracks. We had been hearing gunfire outside the wire for some days, and that night the staccato *rat-a-tat-a-tat* was being joined by the deep booming of artillery landing nearby.

We lay on our cots with our eyes open, as the barracks roof shook from the bombs. I had no idea who was doing the shooting, or why, but we could tell that the officers were becoming increasingly agitated as the report of explosions sounded closer and closer to the camp.

Then the call came. The platoon commanders rushed into the barracks and told us that there was a general evacuation. There was no plan for escape, we should just grab what we could hold in our hands and run where there didn't appear to be shooting.

When I got out of the camp I could see tracer fire over-head, and the flash of artillery explosions illuminating the night. Boys ran in all directions, but we mostly ran west, towards Sudan. I ran west.

I know now that the forces that nearly overran our camp were Eritreans fighting for independence from Ethiopia. As we were allies of the Ethiopian government, the Eritreans would have not considered it a waste of bullets to shoot SPLA recruits.

I ran through the night with the bulk of the crowd towards the border. When I got to the bank of the Gilo River, the rough border mark between the two countries, there was a glut of boys looking backwards and forwards manically at two terrible fates. In front of them was a black blanket of water rushing, peaking and roaring a terrible roar. Behind them were the Eritrean troops, who were now obviously intent on giving chase and were firing at us.

Despite being a fisherman's son who had lived on the Nile, I, like most of the boys, was yet to learn to swim. John had tried to teach me just before I was taken into the army, but I had disappeared from his grip while he was spurring me to kick my feet, and ended up sinking. It took him quite a few moments to find me again and not before I had roiled and rolled underneath the canopy of the Nile and developed a hatred of being underwater.

A rope had been strung across the Gilo to help the boys cross, but it had broken, sending some boys on it under the dark wet surface. Some emerged and made it to the bank. Some didn't. A second rope was being strung, but the sound of gunfire was getting closer and closer.

When I entered the river I clamped both hands on the rope, gripping with fear. It was only adrenaline that allowed me to let go with my rear hand and hold on with my front hand. By the time I got to the Sudanese side of the river, I looked back to see the Eritreans were fighting the SPLA rear guard, and the boys who couldn't swim had thrown themselves into the river anyway and were flailing around.

When there were no more Sudanese on the Ethiopian side of the Gilo, the Eritreans stopped firing and started screaming at us in Arabic.

We stopped and stared. In the moonlight I saw that the advancing troops were mostly women, and they were flashing their private parts at us.

The screaming continued, coalescing into a chant.

You were chased away by pussy.
You were chased away by pussy.
You were chased away by pussy.

We rushed back into Sudan before these mad women could follow us, but the structure of our units had broken down. Some went south, but most of us went west, retracing our steps back to Pachella, where a refugee camp had been established.

When I entered that camp I became, for the first time in my life, a legitimate refugee and found that a refugee's life was indistinguishable from that of a soldier in waiting.

The months after fleeing Ethiopia were very lean indeed. There were no *kawaja* in blue hats, and no *digigstralia* in the camp at Pachella. Most of us survived on whatever bush fruit we could scavenge. Once again us boys became thin and sickly, especially the boys who ate the wrong fruits. More started to die.

Then, one day, planes flew over the camp and threw cargo at us. Too weak to run from the planes, we just watched the shapes float down towards us. We were happy to find that the cargo didn't explode, and ecstatic to find that it was crates of wheat and medicine. The wheat was not *digigstralia,* but we were in no position to be picky.

I gained some of my bulk back when the *kawaja* started dropping food into the Pachella camp, and then lost it all again when disease swept through the camp and my fever and weakness returned.

I have already described sickness, so I will not repeat it, but once again the meat fell from my bones, fever gripped my mind, and death called. Then, at the height of my sickness, when I was wondering once again if I was destined to be stitched into a corn sack, I was placed on the back of a small plane and flown to a military hospital in a South Sudanese town called Kapoeta for treatment.

I can only assume that it was a family member in the higher ranks of the SPLA who managed my transfer, but I have never been able to identify whom it was that arranged that flight. I suspect I owe my life to him.

Even though Kapoeta was in a fertile part of the country, and on the Singaita River, the town looked like a desert. All of the trees near and in the city had been destroyed by fire or design, so there was no cover for anyone trying to attack or defend.

A town of great strategic importance, Kapoeta had been taken and retaken a number of times already during the war, so everyone in the town was on tenterhooks.

When I had recovered from my sickness, I was moved from a hospital to military barracks in Kapoeta, and was surprised to find it full of familiar faces. I learned that, shortly after I had been airlifted out of Pachella, planes and helicopters from the northern-controlled government bombed the refugee camp, before seizing the town.

After a couple of weeks in the crowded barracks, government planes started to arrive at Kapoeta. Amidst heavy bombing, we fled that town. Shortly after, it once again fell to the government, with many deaths on both sides.

After Kapoeta we walked through the bush to a town called Kedipo, and there my brother John once again crossed my path. The SPLA were attempting to take Juba, the largest city in the south, and John, then a radio operator, was to be part of a bolstering force.

John was stunned to see that I was still alive. He had heard that I'd been killed. We only spoke for a short while, each explaining how the war raged around us. Both of us had seen cousins on our travels, and both of us had seen them committed to the ground.

We were both very sick. John had scars from bombs and bullets, and something poisonous had bitten his foot, making it balloon up to twice its normal size. We were alive, though, both of us. That fact seemed like a miracle.

'I hope to see you again, little Deng,' he said to me with as much tenderness as is possible for someone in the middle of a war. He said more, but that's all I remember of it. I remember watching him hobbling off, and I remember hoping that one day I would see him again.

The government bombers came to Kedipo shortly after that meeting with John, and it quickly became apparent that it too would fall to the Arabs. As far as we knew, there was only one more place to flee to: a town named Torit.

Torit was a town that the northerners perhaps hated more than any other. It was the home of the first Anyanya Rebellion in 1955, when Southern soldiers turned on their Sudan Defence Force officers, and disappeared into the bush. Furthermore, everyone knew that the famous and ferocious Kuol Manyang Juuk commanded the garrison at Torit. I had never met this man, but he was a relative of mine and, at the time, I was proud to be related to a man who so enthusiastically prosecuted the war.

Torit was a fertile town, with abundant mango, coconut and fig trees. Pressed close against the border with Kenya, it also had no shortage of goods coming in and out. If the tide were ever to turn in the war, it felt to me it would happen in a town like Torit, and so we were happy to arrive there. But a few days after our arrival the town started being bombed with a ferocity I'd not seen before.

Every day, giant Antonov An-24 and An-26 transport planes, heavy with crudely made barrel bombs, lumbered over the town before releasing their loads and soaring away, light and free. We would wait for the whistle, and the boom and the searing jagged metal.

I have a strong memory of one of the air raids – the second of that day. I was running with another man to a hole in the ground when a bomb landed close to us. I saw the man's body continue to run without his head, which had been sheared off by shrapnel.

The headless body seemed to keep running for some seconds, before it fell limp into the mud. I suppose it must have been a trick of the mind.

Those were long, dangerous days in Torit. There was nowhere else to go, though, so we scavenged food, ran from bombs and hoped that the SPLA units elsewhere were making gains.

We heard bad things about the Juba offensive. People said that the government soldiers were repelling the attacking SPLA, and that a great number of our soldiers had been killed. Then I learned, from a distant uncle also sheltering in Torit, that John had been killed in the fighting.

I was sad when I heard the news, but my sadness was mitigated by the fact that I didn't expect to live much longer anyway. With no protection from the planes, our numbers were slowly thinning and I assumed that we would all die from bombs, or the offensive that would surely come soon.

Then a group of new SPLA soldiers came to Torit – older soldiers, some quite fat. They started to order those of us boys remaining who had been trained in Pinyudo into the nearby Imatong Mountains in Eastern Equatoria, a region of South Sudan. Older boys and men organised the trek. We took what food we could scrounge and said our goodbyes to the old men and women we'd been sheltering with and started off on another journey.

Some of our trip was on open plains, but some was across near-impenetrable ground, and dense forest. The trip also took us through areas controlled by the Toposa and Lotuko people – tribes that at that time were aligned with the northern-controlled government. Though we were being marched by armed and experienced soldiers, many boys and soldiers lost their lives in hit-and-run guerilla attacks.

Some of the killings would have been politically or tribally motivated, but most were just gun robberies, with the soldiers losing their weapons, ammunition and lives when they dropped off the pack to urinate or rest.

Most of us boys survived the trip, which took several weeks, and we finally arrived at a tiny mountain town called Ameh, near the Ugandan border. We found it swollen by hundreds – perhaps thousands – of my fellow Dinka-Bor who were living in a hastily made camp.

I wondered why so many of my people chose to be so far from the Nile, until I started to hear the stories. Thousands of people had died, it seemed, losing their lives on the blades of sharp tools or bludgeons. Our cows had been indiscriminately slaughtered, and the *luaks* and dams and fields had been burned or destroyed. There was rape too, which I now understood, and not only of the living.

This had all happened over just a few days, and now more than 100,000 of my people had abandoned their villages. Many of them were sheltering in Ameh, because it was one of the last places that my people felt safe.

I thought about my mother.

As I listened to more stories, I was told that it was not Arabs who had decimated my people, but ghosts – man- and boy-shaped apparitions with ash on their faces and death on their minds.

Of course it was not ghosts that actually did the killing. It was men and boys. It's always men and boys. The killers were part of a faction of the SPLA consisting mostly of people from the Nuer tribe, the second largest ethnic group in South Sudan after the Dinka.

Most of the killers had been SPLA soldiers who had mutinied when Nuer officers called for Dr John Garang to be deposed and replaced with the well-liked Nuer commander Riek Machar. They were calling themselves the SPLA-Nasir, named after Machar's base town, with their shock forces being a group of older Nuer boys who called themselves the 'White Army'. It was this last force that had enthusiastically conducted most of the massacres in and near my village.

Many of the White Army were killing my people to help fulfil a prophecy foretold by a nineteenth-century Nuer prophet Ngundeng Bong. Ngundeng Bong claimed that a left-handed man would take over the world, and Riek Machar's spiritual advisor, a man named Wurnyang, was convinced that Machar was that left-handed man. The conquering of the world was to start with a massacre near my village.

In the weeks that followed, more and more scattered war boys were delivered to Ameh. They had come from throughout the south, with some walking for months. When it looked like no more boys were coming, we were all brought together for one last journey, before joining the fight.

Like most of the boys at that stage, I was more than ready to report for duty. We had been homeless for so long; we'd been hunted and bombed and chased from town to town. We'd seen small massacres and heard of very large ones. Now we thought we had an opportunity to have our voices heard.

We all missed our mothers and fathers – not the woman and man who had made our lives possible, but the steel and the leader that would make our enemies' deaths possible. We all had the black tar of hatred stuck to our insides. We were ready to kill.

From Ameh we were marched to a garrison town named Moli, and into a military base like the one in Ethiopia. There we were assigned new squads. All of us boys from broken units around the south were now reconstituted as the Red Army.

I was ready to learn to fight and kill in that base, but for some reason it was not to be. I don't know why, but we were left in Moli without weapons or training.

As was seemingly the case for any camp where we were left to stagnate, parasites and disease ran rampant through us. Jiggers were everywhere and some of the boys ended up permanently crippled after the creatures made their way deep into their bodies via some wound or cavity. One boy in my unit even lost his penis after a colony of jiggers set up camp in his urethra.

Once again I was living in a familiar misery. The only framework of our day was military discipline and disgusting, meagre rations.

It seemed the camp was in disarray due to the Dinka–Nuer split, which was decimating the SPLA. Government forces routinely attacked the supply lines from the fields near the Nile to the mountain bases, but sometimes there were no supplies to transport anyway as the civil war within a civil war suffered endless tit-for-tat atrocities, killing farmers or pushing them from their lands.

In Moli we were given a handful of rotting sorghum grains each day, but they were not fit for a dog to eat. The grains could only be eaten after they were boiled in water and bush herbs, and even after getting that foul mix into our bellies, those grains weren't finished doing harm.

Almost every boy got sick after each meal, with most of us becoming constipated. Some boys got so sick they were taken to the field hospital, and the rest of us had to manually void our bowels by going into the forest, finding a long, straight stick and scooping out the shit.

The trees with the most appropriate branches were found by following the trails of dried blood and excrement.

In Moli there were both Dinka and Nuer conscripts in the camp, and there was no apparent disharmony between us until, one day, gunfire erupted. I don't know what prompted the fighting, but after the shooting finished most of the Nuer recruits disappeared into the bush.

From that moment those boys, many of whom I had shared the long journey from Pinyudo to Moli with, became my enemy. The war between Dinka and Nuer was to intensify in 1992 and Nuer commanders tried to turn the untrained boys into a guerilla force capable of attacking SPLA bases in the mountains. But the handful of green boys were no match for the hardened soldiers and the wannabe Nuer commandos were almost all slaughtered.

They were my enemy, but I couldn't help but feel sad every time I heard of another easy routing of the Nuer boys.

As the war within a war worsened, conditions at Moli deteriorated. Even the hated sorghum became scarce, and there were often overlapping outbreaks of disease. Soon more than a dozen boys were dying every day. As a fighting unit, the losses were making us combat ineffective, without us ever having faced the real enemy.

The SPLA recognised this fact, so everyone who was able was marched higher into the mountain range, to a town called Chukudum, which was now the centre of

SPLA operations. While northern forces occupied Juba, Chukudum would be the capital of free South Sudan.

When we walked into Chukudum, we got a sense of how fragile the rebellion had become. There was a strong military presence – soldiers, tanks and other vehicles of war – but it didn't have a sense of permanence. Even Dr John Garang's headquarters comprised only a slightly larger tent than the rest.

The SPLA had chosen Chukudum as its base because it was remote and easily defensible, but also because of the turbulence created by the mountains nearby, which meant the government bombers didn't have a complete free rein over the area. Bombs still landed nearby, but rarely where they were directed.

In this mountain base, Dr John Garang hatched a plan to turn the war around. The government had made gains too quickly, and to garrison every town they had seized would have required an army much larger than the one the SPLA had. They figured those towns could be retaken, and if they took them around April or May they wouldn't need to defend them because the ensuing months of rain would make it almost impossible for the government to move enough cavalry, artillery and troops to retake them. A large offensive was planned for strategically important towns.

While the south was a kingdom of mud, the SPLA would build defences, resupply from across the border, and establish vicious militias consisting of local tribes. Dr Garang believed the course of the war could be turned around with a relatively small collection of shock troops deployed at the right time, augmented with the right tribal alliances in strategic towns. Torit and Kapoeta would be key, with those towns being the doorways to Uganda and Kenya respectively.

An essential part of the plan, however, was collecting the scattered soldiers-in-waiting like me from around the south, and getting them through intensive training so they could conduct these offensives. For this plan to come into effect, there would have to be new, protected training camps in the hills so, after a very short amount of time in Chukudum, we were sent to a clearing which would become a training camp called Nattinger.

Once again I was making bush tents and carving out paths, but this time it was with purpose and urgency. As soon as the basic structures of the camp at Nattinger were done, Dr John Garang visited us and gave a speech about the importance of our work.

As Dr Garang gave his speech, a group of fat, healthy soldiers in special uniforms eyed us boys and the bush behind us. These were Dr Garang's personal bodyguards, and part of a dangerous special force known as the Bright Star Campaign (BSC or Commandos). One set of BSC eyes landed on me while scanning the crowd, and stayed there. I met the man's gaze and was surprised to find familiarity.

This man was a cousin of mine by the name of William Deng Malou Akau whom I'd last seen in my mother's *luak*. He was one of the Anyanya fighters who had helped repel the Arabs who had come to attack my village. After Dr Garang's speech, he strode up to me.

'You have become big, Deng Athieu. Almost a man,' he said.

The food in Nattinger was a vast improvement over what we'd been given in Moli, but I was not that much bigger than I had been at age seven. I was taller, certainly, but not much bigger.

'You will be a soldier soon,' he continued.

'I hope so,' I said. I meant it too. I had been floating on the winds of the war but as a soldier I felt like I would have weight.

Then I experienced perhaps the first moment of happiness in some years when this cousin, painted with reflected leadership celebrity, bade me wait until he brought a full set of uniform khakis. I was too small for the uniform, but I would grow into it. I had never been so proud, and had never been so intent to fulfil the promise of Dr John Garang's plans.

I would be a soldier. I would make my father happy, and I would also make my mother happy.

I trained for weeks with a wooden rifle, until I was finally given the essential tools of a soldier: a unique SPLA number, the badges that would identify me as one of Dr Garang's fighters, and the most important tool any revolutionary in Africa – in fact almost any revolutionary in the world since the start of the Cold War – needs. I was given my very own selective automatic Kalashnikov 7.62 millimetre, gas-operated rifle, usually known as an AK-47.

Now I was ready to kill.

From when I first saw soldiers in my village as a boy, I'd known that the AK-47 was a manifestation of power. From the moment I started training with the SPLA, I'd known that the rifle was an essential part of effective soldiering.

We were also issued a commodity more important than grain or water – handfuls of steel-cased 7.62 millimetre cartridges.

Once we started our live ammunition training, our conditions improved again. Even then I knew this was because our value was increasing. Every time we fired a round, the SPLA was investing in us. If we died of disease or starvation at that point, it would have cost them more than just the sweat of digging a grave.

Like the rest of the boys, I was terrified when I first pulled the trigger of my rifle. The shudder of recoil jolted my hands and almost dislocated my shoulder, the crack of the round escaping the barrel hurt my ears, and I was scared of having the bullet fly anywhere but the target in front of me. After a few weeks of live firing, I stopped being terrified and started feeling empowered. I started to believe that death only happened in front of our weapons. Behind me was only strength.

I was becoming somebody, and I liked it.

I had my rifle with me at all times. It was my life. I couldn't wait to point it at the enemy and, calmly and deliberately, depress the trigger and watch the Arab bodies fall. Strangely, it was also at that camp that I started to change my opinion of the Arabs, who we'd been schooled to believe were the enemy.

Just below our camp were barracks where captured northern fighters were kept. Collectively we called them Arabs, but most of them were Darfurian or Nubian, and many were just as dark-skinned as us.

You may think that the northerners would have been treated very poorly at that prisoner-of-war camp, but they weren't treated that differently from us boys, except that, at the end of the day, they were taken to their barracks and locked inside. They were fed, and they had water and rest because they, like us, had a value. In fact, perhaps they had more value than us, as many of them were skilled craftsmen, fashioning garments like uniforms and ammunition pouches, as well as helping erect tents and barracks, and designing irrigation systems.

As we trained at Nattinger with terrible vigour, those Arabs walked around the camp with their heads down, doing their jobs. When I saw their weakness, I became increasingly convinced that we were destined to become the warriors that Dr John Garang told us we would become.

It was only as I watched those Arab men – our enemy – that I considered what it would be like to kill the northern men. I thought about specific prisoners I'd seen, and what it would look like to line them up in my sights and watch them fall after I pressed the trigger. I decided that I had no desire to kill the Arabs in the camp, but I would be capable of killing the enemy when the time came.

Then after a couple of months of training in Nattinger, word started to spread around the camp that we were about to be deployed.

I was convinced we were ready. We knew how to attack, we knew how to protect the flank, we knew how to shoot our rifles, and some people even knew how to use the big artillery guns. Some boys knew how to use the radio, and other boys knew how to put a bandage on another boy when he'd been shot. As far as I was concerned, there was no more to know about making war. We were ready to fight.

Before we moved out there was a short ceremony and we were redesignated *Jaysh Azraq*, or the Blue Army – a new force that was tasked with taking back the small part of Eastern Equatoria close to the Kenyan border.

We were marched to a staging camp in the hills near the town of Kapoeta. The town was occupied by government forces and had been subjected to heavy fighting, captured and recaptured many times over since I had fled it.

In the staging camp we were placed under the command of a man named Commander Majok Mach Aluong, and his adjutant Captain Luol.

Majok was perhaps forty years of age, which made him far older than most fighters in the base. Skinny and small, he had a narrow face, which could sharpen even more when he found something he disliked. He was an intense authoritarian, but was also well educated, and I immediately knew he had an innate sense of justice. I liked him a lot.

Captain Luol was a few years younger than Majok, and a much bigger man – certainly more than two metres tall – with broad shoulders, strong arms, and deep tribal scarring across his forehead. He was dynamic and fearsome – the heat to Majok's fire.

The discipline at the camp was extreme, but manageable, because the rules that we lived under were no longer designed to create subservient boys, but powerful soldiers. Initially morale under Majok and Luol was healthy.

Luol was a singer, and he would bring us together sometimes at the end of the day and sing verses of war songs to prepare us for the front line. The songs made us yearn for battle. All we wanted from life was to have a moment of heroism like the men in Captain Luol's songs. He sang with a power that was commensurate with his frame and his voice would excite us.

Commander Majok would talk to us about what the virtues of a good soldier were. He would also tell us about the myriad enemies that we could encounter in battle. It was not only Arabs who were our enemies, but also cowardice. We must also be wary of the lesser tribes. They were not to be trusted, but sometimes must be cooperated with.

Knowing that we would be deployed near Kapoeta, Majok and Luol had decided to try and gain favour with a fierce, war-loving local tribe called the Toposa.

During the war, the Toposa were sometimes strategically aligned with the SPLA, and sometimes aligned with the government, depending on how the relationship could be turned into wheat or weapons. Inside Toposa lands they could be a formidable force multiplier for us. When they were aligned with us they would harass government troops and kill from within. When they were not, they were as terrifying as the Murle.

To keep the Toposa onside Commander Majok and Captain Luol created a commonality of conflict. The Toposa had no real, deep-seated hatred for the SPLA or the government – they killed only because it suited their immediate purposes – but they had a genuine detestation for an adjacent cattle-herding tribe called the Didinga.

For generations the Toposa had been warring with the Didinga, usually over cattle grazing rights, but often over revenge and ancient slight. The conflict had been particularly extreme since the mid-1970s, when the Didinga returned to Sudan from a decade of exile in Uganda. In Uganda, the tribe had been exposed to new forms of large-scale farming and education, which they now expected to have in South Sudan. The Toposa saw both as a threat to the natural order of the area.

When the civil war came to the area, and it was flushed with death and weaponry, these tribal hatreds escalated. Understanding this well, Commander Majok sent word around the area that Toposa men could come to our base to receive grain and ammunition if they brought us a severed head of a Didinga tribesman.

The heads came in daily, and it was left to us boys to inspect them. They were usually marked with a hangdog, and yet also shocked, expression. When we found the tribal scarring and tooth extraction that denoted a Didinga man, we'd approve the distribution of a few clips of 7.62 millimetre ammunition or a bag of grain or wheat.

Bonds of brutality between the Toposa tribesmen and us were created in that base, and our leaders hoped these bonds would be useful for us when we reached the battlefield.

From that base above the front line, we boys took turns conducting patrols around the area. We relished those missions. We would be out in the bush, with our weapons, looking for spies or enemies; it was the closest thing we'd done yet to actual soldiering.

One day, six of us were sent out on patrol, and I was happy to find that I had been sent out of the wire with an artilleryman a couple of years older than me named Numeri, who was a good friend.

Numeri was shorter than me, but very squat and powerful, and he was both a natural leader and someone who brought levity to the sometimes long, hot and arduous patrols. He would joke when it was time to joke, and get us to concentrate when that was called for, and he was the best at hunting out tasty bush foods when our stomachs grumbled.

Numeri had a particularly acute eye for hives filled with honey. On this particular patrol he spotted a hive high in a tree, climbed up and had just brought his hand, covered with honey, up to his face when a single bullet from a sniper's rifle pierced his hand, nose and then brain. By the time he landed, he was already dead.

I scooped up Numeri's body and carried it back to the base. When Captain Luol saw this dead boy, he raged with fury.

He hollered that this was a Didinga revenge attack, and that the man who had killed one of ours needed to be found and brought to us. Even though we thought it unlikely that we would be able to find the Didinga sniper, we enthusiastically supported the idea of a brutal retaliation.

Numeri was our friend. He had done no wrong, or so we thought. We also felt that the attack had been cowardly.

A few days later, in a moment of extreme fortune or misfortune depending on your perspective, one of our scouts spied a large group of Didinga tribespeople – most likely a family – moving past the base.

We were sent out to grab them. Although they were wary of us, they certainly had no idea of the danger we represented because they neither ran nor put up a fight.

Instead, they just let us take them into our camp, like cattle being led to an unknown fate.

The group was carrying a small amount of panned gold, which we assumed they were on their way to sell in Kenya. They were men and women, and children, and even a pregnant woman, and we tortured all of them terribly. We called it an interrogation, but even I knew that they knew nothing about Numeri and the sniper who killed him.

We hogtied them – wrists trussed to their ankles – and dumped them in a hole in the middle of the hot sun that day. Without water or shade, they wriggled in increasing pain as the hours went on. We screamed at them, asking endlessly about Numeri. They tried to appease us but couldn't as they had none of the information that we wanted.

This went on throughout the day and into the evening, until we were all tired from the interrogation and we went to the barracks to sleep. When we woke in the morning, the bodies of the Didinga people were ruined. Some could no longer move their arms and legs, and some had passed out from the pain and couldn't elicit any response except a croak or a groan. I wondered what would happen to them.

Mid-morning, a group of us were sent off on patrol to one of the artillery positions just outside the camp. On the path to the gun position, we met with a unit of

Commandos heading back to our base. I knew their arrival had something to do with the Didinga people.

We were not experienced torturers, but the Bright Star Campaign men certainly were. Perhaps they could gain some information about Numeri's killer.

As we returned from an uneventful patrol, my nose was filled with good smells. I said to the group that it seemed there had been a successful hunt in our absence; perhaps we would be filling our bellies with barbecued meat when we got back to the camp.

An older boy who had no nose – he had accidentally shot himself – laughed grotesquely.

'You think a meal will be greeting you when you get back to the camp?' he said. 'We will see. We will see.'

I was so naive.

When we arrived at the camp, the BSC had done their work and left. Thirteen smouldering bodies were still filling the air with the smell of cooking. The bodies were white and grey and pink and black, and their skin had started peeling away. Their faces had melted and their hair was gone, as well as their breasts and genitals. The pregnant woman's belly burned fiercely, sometimes sending little blue and yellow spirals upwards.

My ears were filled with the sound of crackling fire, and also the wheezes and whistles as the air in the bodies expanded and escaped. Every so often I heard the howl of a hyena, excited by the smell of meat. That smell – which had a few minutes before seemed welcome and inviting – started to choke my throat, and turn my belly.

Then, after a short period, I started to feel fine. My stomach was normal, and so too seemed my mind. I wondered if this was what it was to be a soldier.

We had killed these people, but it didn't matter. There was so much death around, it did not matter how or why it came, nor even really to whom. If it were not us making the death, it would have been the Toposa, or the Nuer, or perhaps the government, or one of the sicknesses, or hunger.

'We were all dead anyway,' I thought. 'It was just that some of us didn't know it yet.' The death of these people only mattered if they affected the prosecution of the war. Their deaths didn't affect the war so they didn't matter at all. Or so I thought.

It was the boy with the missing nose who noticed that there were thirteen bodies burning on the ground, not the fourteen we had captured. There was a frantic backtracking over the last few hours.

It seems that the BSC had arrived and decided all of the Didinga should be executed. Instead of spending fourteen cartridges, the BSC used the butts of their rifles to knock the Didinga unconscious, hitting them on the back of their necks, just below their skulls. Then wood was collected and a pyre was built. The unconscious bodies were then thrown onto the fire, but it seems that one of the men was not struck hard enough and had disappeared into the bush.

A patrol was immediately convened, which I was a part of. We were to track, find and then kill this man. He would have been injured from the torture and the beating, so we figured we should be able to find him.

We spent two days and two nights hunting this man. We found his trail a number of times, but ultimately he managed to evade us. This Didinga man's story is an unlikely and exceptional tale of survival and I commend him on it. He is the hero of another story.

After evading us, this Didinga man connected with his people, and then journeyed to Chukudum, where his tribal leaders and Bishop Taban confronted Dr John Garang himself. The SPLA was attempting to present itself as a legitimate government-in-waiting, so the official response in Chukudum was one of outrage.

The man was given an apology, and was told that punishment would be meted out to the perpetrators.

The punishment doled out to us was, in some ways, extreme, and in another way completely inconsequential.

The SPLA ordered that our unit was to be sent to the bloody front line against the government soldiers in Kapoeta. It's what was designed for us all along, and the thing that we had craved for some years, but it's easy to see it as a punishment too, as few of the boys survived the ensuing battles.

I was eleven years old.

Chapter Five

APPOINTMENT IN KAPOETA

Before we moved out for Kapoeta, a large group of recruits arrived. They were boys I recognised from Pinyudo. While the rest of us fled west to Sudan after crossing the Gilo River to avoid the Eritrean attack, these boys, led by some SPLA soldiers, fled south, ending up at a refugee camp called Kakuma in Kenya.

You would need no more than a few days in Kakuma to learn about most of the woes of East Africa of the time. You could approach men from Burundi to hear about the Hutu massacres, or Tutsi massacres. If you approached the Ethiopian men, you would hear about socialist atrocities, or nationalist atrocities. Somali and Eritrean men would also tell you of fighting and death, as would Rwandan and Congolese men. The women would tell you stories of rape, or of dead and sick children, or both.

For East Africa, it was a time of fighting, massacre and rape. But not in Kakuma in Kenya, where there was no war. And yet these boys had come home. They'd heard the call of Dr John Garang – a song of rebellion and independence – and their ears had decided they needed to get closer to that music. They were our brothers.

We knew that they were with us when we heard their voices, full and strong, singing the war songs that Captain Luol led us in. As their mouths expertly worked around the angular Arabic of the songs, we knew they must have been singing them even while they were across the border.

'*Walid jonub ma bicub yom chakel,*' Luol would sing.

The sons of the south never fear on the day of the battle.

'*NAM! NAM!*' We would holler.

YES! YES!

'*Ana reujjel chela ne mud, malu?*'

We are men. If we die, so what?

That line was for the officers and boys alike.

When we were all back together – both the boys who had committed the atrocity against the Didinga, and the new boys from Kakuma – we marched to a town called

Lotouke, where we would be armed and then taken to the front line.

At Lotouke there were gifts waiting for us from nearby nations, like Uganda and Ethiopia, who either had a love for the SPLA, or a hatred for Khartoum. There was stack upon stack of AK-47 rifles; boxes of belt-fed machine guns; serpentine reams of long, sharp rounds; rocket launchers; and stocky mortars with their toy-like ammunition. There were trucks and Land Rovers, some of which had been opened with saws, like a can, so that the seats could be extracted and replaced with the larger guns. There were also giant CAT vehicles, which could transport troops across muddy roads on the fringes of the wet season.

The potency in these armaments and their explosive power bled into us, and we started to become wild. We had been eating, so we were strong; we had been training, so we were fierce; and we were boys, so we were rebellious. We had already seen death, and no longer feared it, so we were also dangerous.

In Lotouke it felt as though our AK-47s started to vibrate, and the rounds strained to escape the clip. We all started to sleep with our weapons, and I would caress the barrel and stock of my gun at night, before dreaming of a time when my rifle and I could fulfil our destinies of death.

We started to hunt with our rifles, which was at odds with the explicit orders of our superiors. We killed many of the four-legged animals of the area with the efficiency of hunters who had been trained to aim, anticipate and execute.

I was effective from about fifty or sixty metres when hunting with my weapon, but there was one twelve-year-old boy from my platoon named Nyilo who was lethal from a much greater distance.

I have never seen a shot like Nyilo. That boy seemed to have a supernatural ability to guide a round into a target, and he enjoyed the currency his skill bought.

Once, when hunting in Lotouke, I killed a small antelope at the very limit of my range. As we skinned the animal, and made a fire, there was great praise of the shot, and many thanks for the meal we were preparing. Nyilo also praised my marksmanship, until he spied, off in the middle distance, a much larger beast.

'I will show you something now, Deng. The true marksman can kill without even leaving a wound.'

He fired two shots in quick succession, one that was fired high to scare the animal, and the second, only a heartbeat after the first.

The animal fell after the shots.

We ran over to the catch, and the antelope was dead as promised. As we ran our hands over the animal there was no apparent wound, either, just as promised.

We asked in disbelief how Nyilo had killed magically, but he would not speak, holding only a knowing smile. The riddle was answered when blood started to leak from the animal's rear.

The first shot had caused the gazelle to turn from the shot, and the second had pierced the animal's anus as it tried to escape.

Our journey back to the camp was full of song: with rhyming tales of death and courage bouncing through the trees. We expected to come into the camp as heroes, with meat enough for our whole platoon, but our cruel Sergeant Major, Garang Akudum, intercepted what was meant to be a triumphal parade.

'WHAT DO I SEE?' he hollered.

The boys scattered, but I, who was heavy with a carcass, could not disappear so easily. Sergeant Major Akudum grabbed me and took me to a shed where he beat me so badly I pissed blood. I was locked in that shed, and in the darkness, I thought only of killing and revenge.

All the boys hated Sergeant Major Akudum, not only because he was a sadist, but also because he was a traitor. Everyone knew that he siphoned off our rations so he could trade them for sex with tribal women nearby. He did the wrong thing by us, and he did the wrong thing by Dr John Garang.

When I was let out of the shed, I went straight to my barracks, and loaded up my weapon. The boys followed as I hunted Sergeant Major Akudum, with the safety off and a round in the chamber. When I saw him I ran at him, pursued by men and boys.

It was a comical scene of running and threats and shouting. I got two shots off before I was disarmed and beaten. Sadly, neither bullet went into the sergeant major, instead they embedded into a tree he was hiding behind.

I was put back into the shed, but in the darkness I did not regret what I had tried to do. I was released after less than a day and my weapon was returned after I promised not to try to kill any more superior officers. The general consensus seemed to be that the sergeant major had it coming.

My incident was only one of many like that in Lotouke. Boys who are given bloodlust, impunity and weaponry are always going to be a danger to all who they encounter, especially when *khat* – a stimulant that, when chewed, creates a similar effect to speed or meth – is introduced. *Khat* suppresses appetite, fuels the blood and tricks the brain. We chewed it almost all day, every day.

During the time we spent in Lotouke, we physically got no closer to the front, but mentally we inched nearer.

We would show our fearsome intent by walking around the camp with the safety switch off our rifles, and a round in the chamber. This often resulted in boys accidentally shooting themselves, or their squad mates, so many of the boys – including me – ended up putting a round in the chamber with the trigger depressed, creating a deliberate jam that could not be perceived by the other soldiers we were trying to threaten. After all, it was not sad to die, but it would have been sad to die so tantalisingly close to the front line without having fought.

In our stimulated haze, we could think of, and talk about, nothing but death, valour, glory and the front line. Killing became an addiction that could not be adequately serviced so, for some boys, death became an acceptable substitute.

Many nights we would be woken by a single shot, usually fired by a boy who had wrapped his mouth around the barrel of his rifle and depressed his thumb against the trigger. It was a strange thing. The boys who did that would go to bed with hearts as full of cause and fury as the rest of us, and then, sometime in the night, they had decided that they could not wait for the battlefield to die.

We didn't mourn those boys. We did not think less of them either. They were just dead.

Ana reujjel chela ne mud, malu?

We are men. If we die, so what?

More and more ammunition was being trucked into Lotouke for the planned assaults ahead, and most days we siphoned off 7.62 millimetre cartridges. We planned to trade them with some local tribesmen, who said they would swap ammunition for food.

On the day of the planned trade, we told some older boys, who had been in Lotouke for some time, about our plan. They warned us that the local men would likely betray us, and kill us as soon as we handed over the ammunition. It had happened before, and would probably happen again.

We could almost taste the extra grains in our mouths though, so we quickly came up with a plan: we would boil most of the bullets, leaving only a couple at the top of one clip, which we would fire off as a tribute to the quality of the rounds. Then, even if they doublecrossed us, we wouldn't be in danger.

When we met the tribesmen, we fired off the two rounds as planned. We handed over the ammunition and they handed over quite a large amount of wheat and sorghum. As soon as we turned our backs, the newly armed men loaded their weapons and tried to kill us. None of the bullets would fire, though. As they looked confusedly at their inanimate weapons, we laughed and raised our rifles. We didn't kill them. We considered it, but perhaps because we were laughing so much, the killing mood paused, and did not come back until after the tribesmen had melted back into the bush.

When most of us left Lotouke we were marched to Kor Machi, the final SPLA staging base for the assault on Kapoeta. Our camp sat directly above the town, on a hill, and we could see our goal. It was the town I had run from while government bombs rained down, and a place of such strategic importance that I felt I would be honoured to die attacking it.

Kapoeta and Torit, the doors to supporting nations Kenya and Uganda, were hallowed names for us at that point. Great, bloody battles had happened in those towns, battles that were immortalised in the songs of Captain Luol. As a western child might fantasise about Disneyland, we dreamed of Kapoeta.

We were so close to our dreams.

In Kor Machi, the older soldiers pored over miniatures of the town, while we waited for the green light to attack. Day and night, our artillery roared from a position behind us – loud death flying towards Kapoeta. Day and night, mortars came in at us from the government positions below.

For the most part, their fire was inaccurate and ineffective, except in one instance.

That time, they used the smoke of a cooking fire to triangulate their target and that round came in like an arrow to a bullseye, exploding right next to our cook while he tended to a stew. He was killed instantly, with his intestines leaping into his bubbling pot. There was an order issued afterwards that there would be no more cooking, and no more fires.

The skies were blue in the days before the assault, but our commanders knew that soon the clouds would come, and with them the rain. The movement of men and machines would be severely hampered then. If the SPLA were to take Kapoeta, it would have to happen very soon. Our commanders knew that, and the Arabs would have known it too. The upcoming fight could be felt in the air.

•

After almost a week in Kor Machi, we were called to conduct our first raid. Our platoon commander, Manute Chin Ayuael, a man who had been training us since Nattinger, told us we were to take our positions.

'I have trained you very well, and I'm sure none of you will die before you have fulfilled your destiny,' he boomed.

There were more roars than cheers.

'Are you all ready to die?' he asked, with a glint in his eye.

'*NAM! NAM! NAM! NAM! NAM!*' we all replied.

That word followed us as we marched on Kapoeta. At a point in the bush, Captain Luol hissed that we should all shut up, and crouch, and wait. We could see the buildings of the town below us, and we couldn't wait to be in combat. There was no fire coming in, nor any going out, but the thrumming in my chest was easily as powerful as any artillery.

We waited, crouched in that long grass for an eternity, until we saw what we were waiting for – Bright Star Campaign commandos. Strong, tall and with expressions of pure determination, they strode towards the town. My pounding heart filled, and it nearly exploded when the sound of heavy machine guns and grenades filled the air.

The battle had begun, and soon we were called to join it.

Captain Luol and Commander Majok stood and Majok turned to us with a smile of pure ecstasy.

'IT'S TIME,' he yelled.

Majok and Luol walked forward with an unhurried gait, and we followed in a low-profile crouch, as we'd been taught for such assaults. Soon we could see the buildings ahead, and the muzzle flashes from the machine-gun bunkers and sandbagged windows. Dirt spat at us as rounds came in, and trees splintered and flaked as they were hit by super-sonic shards of metal.

Majok and Luol never flinched or slowed as they walked towards the town, even though tracers sometimes blasted, like lasers, between them. Majok and Luol had the poise of superheroes. The rounds continued to come in and I wondered if that pair of men could even be penetrated by something as mundane as a bullet.

As we moved ever closer to the town, I could see that there were a number of fights already underway, with the BSC commandos engaging some of the machine-gun nests from cover.

We crawled on, and Majok and Luol strode on, and my heart kept thumping until Luol leaned back on his heels and hollered in an undulating and euphoric voice.

'*HAJUM! HAJUM! HAJUM! HAJUM! HAJUM! HAJUM!*'

Attack! Attack!

We had been waiting for the call so we leapt up from our crouching positions and sprinted as quickly as we could at the town below. Guns that weren't already engaged turned to us and started to fire. I often heard a whiz when a round made its way from Kapoeta, but every so often there was a crack, as though the bullet was shattering air. I will forever know the difference between rounds fired near me, and rounds fired at me.

We ran as fast as our legs could take us, screaming with bloody intent, zig-zagging in the way we had been trained to do. I could see the faces of the enemy now, those Arabic invaders who had come to our lands to steal away our way of living, if not our lives. None of them were of Arab descent though – they were all Nubian or Darfurian, many likely press-ganged into the northern army, and all almost as black as I was.

But these men were still the enemy, and they were firing at us. When I was within effective range, I picked a window with a machine gun poking from it, planted my feet as I had been trained, raised my rifle and started to fulfil my sacred destiny.

The rounds from my gun spat at the machine gunners with all the accuracy I could manage. The bullets in my clip disappeared quickly, so I advanced my position and, behind a tree, I went down on one knee and popped in a second clip. *Cla-CLACK*. I was whole again.

My first mission was half over, as this raid was just an exploratory one. We were to sweep across enemy positions, and expose the hidden machine-gun nests in the buildings and bunkers. When identified, the spotters behind us were to relay the firing positions to the artillerymen at Kor Machi.

When engaged, we were told not to dig in, but to move on quickly across the battlefield. We were to be small and nimble, and judicious with what meagre ammunition we had. In retrospect, we were little more than bait.

I started running again and spent my second clip at another position that had opened up on our platoon. Soon my feet had thumped on enough dirt torn up by bullets and artillery that I was on the edge of the bush again, and in a position of defilade from the machine guns. I was out of range and safe. I could still hear the staccato chattering of enemy guns, but that song was no longer playing for me.

My first battle was over, and far too quickly. Had I killed? I wasn't sure. Was I dead or wounded? After patting my body, I was sure I was not harmed. Was that really all there was to fighting in a war?

I came back from the battle with only snapshots of memory – far-away muzzle flashes, strained enemy faces, and the popping sound of guns. Was there nothing more for me than that? Was I more now than I had been this morning?

I dared myself to go back to the battle, to make sure that I hadn't missed anything. It had been drilled into us that a good soldier must forage in the battlefield, so I thought I would go back out into the field of fire and see if I could retrieve a weapon or some ammunition.

I snuck back in front of the guns. They were still firing, but I could tell by the sound of the fire around me that I was yet to be in any gun's sights. The approach to Kapoeta was littered with bodies, but I couldn't see any weapons or ammunition to snatch. I turned some dead soldiers over to see if they had fallen on something worth foraging, but all I found was flesh and blood, blank stares and open eyes.

Eventually I decided to forage a second uniform, so I found a man roughly the same size as me whose deathblow – a packet of bullets to the chest – had destroyed his life, but not his khakis. I had heard that, at the moment of death, everyone shits in his pants, and as I started to pull the dead man's pants down, I found proof sticking to his arse.

I returned to Kor Machi with no further incident. I wondered if I was now a soldier. I had the weapon, the uniform (two), and combat experience. I had fired at the enemy and had been fired upon. There was only one possible requirement that I most likely had not met, and that was the requirement of killing.

A smell followed me back to Kor Machi – a smell that first came into my nose in Pinyudo when those soldiers had been executed in front of me. Quite a large meal greeted our platoon that night but I could not eat because each bite tasted like that alive–dead smell. Food had been a joy of my childhood, and now it felt that my last possibility of pleasure had been consumed by battle. My hunger has never really returned, and even now I don't enjoy food like I once did.

As the artillery continued to rumble and Majok and Luol planned, we watched, from our spot above the town, and waited for our second bite of combat. Each of us war boys planned, a thousand times, the path of destruction we would take when unleashed again. We had been too eager before, we agreed among us, and we'd also been too timid. Next time we would be methodical, efficient and ruthless. The enemy would not be so fortunate again.

With a head full of battle I had three more nights of rest without sleep, and three more meals without hunger – that smell would not disappear – before it was time for our second assault on Kapoeta.

This was to be a much larger attack. Four whole battalions were activated for the assault, and we were laden with clips of ammunition, and grenades. Last time the plan had been just to engage the machine guns, and then sweep left across the field of fire until we were out of range. This time we were told not to return unless Kapoeta had been taken. For our part, our unit was to advance with the rest and then sweep, as quickly as we could, to the flank, and engage the machine-gun nests there that would still be firing forward. It sounded wonderful to us.

We were called to combat at around midnight, and each platoon commander gave his troops their final instructions, and final words of inspiration.

'Are you ready to kill?' Manute Chin Ayuael said over and over.

'*NAM!*'

Of course we were.

'Are you ready to die?'

'*NAM!*'

'Not before you have killed, my men.'

There was uproarious laughter.

Under the cover of darkness, we approached the town as silently as possible. It was to be a surprise attack, so we were to be attuned to every heavy footfall on the ground, every connection between rifle and buckle, every broken twig and branch. All I could hear was the pounding of my own heart.

We moved extremely slowly through the trees and shrubs on the same approach we had made a few days earlier. This time, though, there were hundreds of SPLA fighters to my left and right. The commanders motioned for us to stop. The darkness of night was still on us, and the attack would come with the first light of the day.

I stared hard at the sky, looking for the milk of the dawn. The thrum of my heart only got heavier. Fantasies ran through my head – of a battlefield littered with dead Arabs and the SPLA flag raised high above the buildings below us.

I looked at the boys around me. Their eyes were wild and wide, and they were unable to focus on anything for more than a moment. I was the same. As the black sky above us took on a tinge of purple, the commanders stood and motioned for us to move again, slowly and silently.

We had been well drilled, and no one rushed forward, or spoke, or coughed or made a sound. We were just a deadly tide ready to drown the enemy occupying the town.

In the pale light, I started to discern the machine-gun positions in front of us. I plotted my run down to the flank. I would have to move in a serpentine fashion to avoid being an easy target for the machine guns, if they were to open up. Perhaps they would not open up, though. Perhaps we could move close enough for our grenadiers to . . .

BOOOOOOM!

One of the boys in front of me was launched skyward by an anti-personnel mine. Before the pieces of the boy had managed to land on the ground, some of the enemy's guns had already opened up. By the time all of the machine guns were firing, the Arab mortars were landing.

The machine guns cut many of the SPLA attackers down instantly and straightaway a large number of us were trying to find a bunker or ditch. There was no cover, though. Majok and Luol stood fast and yelled in Arabic for us to move up, and keep attacking.

Some SPLA machine guns opened up behind us and, with that suppressing fire at our backs, we tried to advance as ordered, but everything went from bad to worse very quickly.

As I ran forward, the battalion to my extreme right ran directly across a minefield. They started to jump and leap like popped corn, with the rattle of explosions coming shortly after, and they were soon combat ineffective.

Then the enemy mortars became more frequent and precise, lighting up the battlefield. The mortars brought with them concussion, heat and sound, which could be heard and felt, left and right, back and forward, and the approach to Kapoeta was soon littered with soldiers and uniforms, and guts and dismembered limbs.

Majok and Luol were still standing steadfast, full of voice and purpose, urging us attackers to continue, but it was becoming physically impossible. There was a squad next to me who was disintegrated when a shell landed in the middle of them.

Guns were cutting boys down to the left and to the right of me. When a machine-gun bullet hits you, you don't react, or fly backwards as you might expect – you just fall down. Many of the boys who had fallen down were not yet dead, but most knew they soon would be. It was a well-known fact that we only collected the walking wounded after our battles, and government troops had no history of taking prisoners.

A shell that landed some metres to my left blew me up into the air. There were boys in my platoon who were blown apart, but I was lucky enough to just be blown up. I stayed intact, but the shrapnel punctured my head, groin and thigh.

Majok and Luol screamed at us to go on. They screamed and screamed and screamed, and I really tried to keep going. Bloody and confused, I ran towards the guns the best I could, but soon every step I took was into an explosion, or direct gunfire.

Of the four batallions trying to assault the town, one had been decimated by mines, one was pinned down by the machine guns and artillery, and another had fled (this batallion was made up exclusively of ethnically diverse conscripts, who were nowhere near as gung-ho as we were). That only left our batallion, which was at less than half strength after just a few minutes of battle.

Fire started coming in from our flanks – single, effective shots aimed at the heads of soldiers who'd managed to find cover. My comrades started to fall dead courtesy of these new snipers. It was Toposa tribesmen firing on us.

I briefly thought about the Didinga dead – the heads and charred corpses – and it seemed unfair that all of that death hadn't even brought us a quantum of loyalty. Perhaps brutality is not how loyalty was earned.

We tried to return fire. We tried to shoot at the Toposa and the government troops, but we were now fighting on too many fronts.

The Toposa were the proverbial fat lady. They only entered a battle when they were convinced an assault would fail, and now they had come to help clear the battlefield so they could loot corpses and gain favours from the government defenders. We were fucked and we all knew it.

Those from my brigade who were still able tried to wheel to the left flank as we'd been ordered, but the attack was over and we were just running away at that point.

I ran towards a tree beyond the range of the machine guns where I saw dozens of SPLA soldiers collecting. A man in my platoon called Peter Raan-Dit was running with me.

'You're bleeding,' Peter Raan-Dit said. Raan-Dit means 'big man' in Dinka.

My head was bleeding, and my body and legs were bleeding. I touched all of the spots where artillery had pierced me, none of the wounds had cut into the inside parts of me.

'No, here,' Peter said, pointing to the small of my back.

When I put my hand there, I found a gouge the size of a coin, and a faucet of blood pouring out. As soon as I felt the bullet wound, I fell to my knees.

'And here,' Raan-Dit said, pointing to my crotch. I grabbed my penis and testicles and found that I had been shot through the balls.

I fell to the ground. I tried to stand, but fell again. Raan-Dit, who was strong and fit, and working as a runner, relaying information from unit to unit, hoisted me over his shoulder and pointed us towards the spot where wounded were being collected.

From Raan-Dit's shoulder, I looked at the battlefield, which was a mess of torn-up dirt, and torn-up men and boys. There were bodies hanging in the trees and in holes in the ground, and there were arms and legs a long way from any of the bodies.

Raan-Dit dropped me amidst a large group of injured and ran back to the battlefield. Within that group of broken soldiers, there was an odd levity. A man who had been shot in the buttocks joked that he hoped he'd be able to shit again, another who had collected a packet of shrapnel in the groin joked he would never be a father.

A man who had suffered many gunshot wounds to the torso asked if we had anything we'd like him to tell God. Another man, who had lost a leg, said the man should tell God to make up a bed for him, because he would last longer than the other man, but not much longer. There was much laughter. I can't remember who died first, but both men were gone within the hour.

Raan-Dit came back with another man, whom he dropped on the ground, and also a story, that he told. He had seen Captain Luol, who had lost both legs to artillery. Raan-Dit said he saw Luol looking at his legs in disbelief before placing his pistol to his forehead and pulling the trigger.

Later, Peter Raan-Dit came back with another wounded man and another story. He had found Commander Majok. He was lying under a tank, shredded by shrapnel wounds. He too was dead.

Raan-Dit came back again and again, always with another injured soldier and more stories, until he did not come back anymore because he had been killed by the machine guns.

There was another SPLA offensive after ours, and that one was successful for a moment. The government machine gunners were killed, and their weapons were seized. Our attackers did not manage to take the enemy mortars, however, because the government troops mounted a counteroffensive, and our people were killed or driven back to Kor Machi.

In the days that followed, the government machine gunners, our boys who walked into the mines, the soldiers who were unlucky with the fall of the artillery, the soldiers who walked into the machine-gun fields, Captain Luol and Commander Majok, and Peter Raan-Dit all slowly rotted into the churned-up earth of the approach to Kapoeta. No bodies were retrieved. It's not what was done in that war.

Eventually a truck arrived at our collection position, and us wounded were stacked in the back, like firewood. Blood mixed, and there were groans and shrieks as the wheels bounced and we were taken, not to Kor Machi, but to Chukudum, where we were driven to a hospital for assessment. In that hospital, the full account of the battle could be seen, heard and smelled.

Combat triage was undertaken. The soldiers with legs and arms clean sheared off would have to wait for treatment, as well as the men who had lost all their skin in fire, and those whose organs had been ruptured, or those who had metal in their guts. Those who had suffered gunshot wounds with small entry wounds, but huge, gaping exit wounds – a hallmark of a Toposa attack, as that was a tribe that liked to file down the tips of their bullets to create a hollow-tip effect – would also have to wait.

Only the soldiers who had a chance of being returned to battle were being treated.

Even though I can still feel my injuries to this very day, it was deemed that they would not preclude me from going back into the fight. My shrapnel wounds and the gaping hole in my balls were stitched up, and a surgeon (not a western surgeon, but a bush mechanic for the body) reached into the wound on my back and pulled out the largest part of the bullet. The smaller parts will perhaps be pulled out one day, but have not been yet.

More wounded arrived, and more, until every inch of every floor of that hospital was covered in bleeding soldiers. Bodies were being carted out every few minutes – the dead or nearly dead – to make way for those who could potentially be re-used. Eventually some of us were taken to trucks and driven to a town called Narus, close to the Kenyan border, and then over the border to Lokichogio.

Although technically part of Kenya – one of the only countries in East Africa where there was no war at the time – there was war in Lokichogio, because the SPLA had brought it there. There were SPLA soldiers everywhere, and the hospital was full of soldiers who'd been wounded in battles in Eastern Equatoria.

I recovered for four weeks at that hospital. There was no bombing in Lokichogio, and there was food and water and also milk, fresh milk, just like the milk I used to drink at Uncle Gongich's cattle camp.

It would have been a good place to be, except that it stank like death. Each day more wounded were piled on the hospital floor, after other dead soldiers were peeled off their crusty mats of blood and buried in mass graves.

I yearned to go back to the front line. I yearned to be out of hospital. There was no fear of death for us boys – we had been indoctrinated too well. As the assault started a small part of me had feared that perhaps there was a lack of courage in me, but I had charged the machine guns, and could again. No, the only real fear in me was of permanent injury, becoming a half-man condemned to a life of begging and pity.

I felt relieved when an SPLA man gave me orders to go back into Sudan. I still had problems walking, but I moved as confidently and strongly as I could, especially when in the presence of officers. Finally, my wish of returning to battle had been answered.

I was crammed in the back of a truck and driven across the border, eventually finding myself back at Nattinger.

I hoped to be reunited with my unit but I found that there was no unit left to join. The Didinga punishment had been realised and most soldiers in my unit – and almost all of us involved in the torture and killings – had been killed or seriously wounded in Kapoeta. I was one of the few to find myself returned to service.

My new unit was called the *moakin* or 'broken unit', partly because it was made up almost exclusively of soldiers from units that had been decimated in actions like the Kapoeta assault, and partly because almost all of us were walking wounded.

The tasks we undertook in Nattinger were menial and dull. We guarded prisoners, undertook recon patrols around the base, delivered bales of cloth and thread to the tailors making uniforms, and helped the mechanics fixing the vehicles that were going back to the front lines.

It was shit work as far as I was concerned. I desperately wanted to go back and fight. The misery of the work was compounded by the fact that I was still in pain every day, and I was suffering bout after bout of fever. We were very removed from the war we were all so invested in, except that sometimes we'd get a sense of morale rising or falling in the officers, or we'd hear battle stories from returned infantrymen.

After months in this painful, sick purgatory, I thought again about ending my own life. I had expected to go back into combat, but it felt like that was never going to happen. It seemed I would end up being the broken man I had so feared becoming.

Chapter Six

RETURN OF JOHN MAC

I was like a ghost in Nattinger, until, after a few months with the *moakin*, my wounds miraculously started to improve, and soon my morale came back. 'Perhaps I will be able to fight again. Perhaps I will still kill Arabs,' I thought.

I started to be able to do more and more karate – a compulsory activity at most SPLA bases – as well as play long games of soccer. I started playing football with a boy of the same age as me named Michael. Michael was not treated well in Nattinger, because there were some rich people in his family and he had avoided fighting in the war. I liked him, though, and not only because he was an exceptional soccer player.

After games, we used to share our experiences and Michael told me about his sister, Elizabeth, who was across the border in Kenya and was married to an SPLA officer named John Mac, which was also my brother's name. This John Mac was from a village near Bor, and he was Dinka-Bor and the same age as my brother.

I told Michael stories of the war, and of my village, and he talked about this brother-in-law, who'd met Michael's sister in the Yita refugee camp in Unity State a few years earlier and then spent more time with her in Kapoeta, where Elizabeth was sheltering after fierce Eritrean women had chased her from a refugee camp in Ethiopia.

When John Mac saw Elizabeth in Kapoeta, he declared that he was going to marry her. A year later, Elizabeth was in a refugee camp in Ameh, near the Kenyan border, and another man threatened to marry her. Hearing this, John Mac rushed to Ameh and married Elizabeth and then was sent back to military duties in the town of Nimule, on the Ugandan border.

Michael was convinced that his brother-in-law was my brother. I knew better than to believe so easily. Untruths were easily told during the war, sometimes because of miscommunication, and sometimes because of wishful thinking. I wouldn't give myself over to a hope. I had heard of my brother John's death many times, and this was the first time that someone had suggested he was alive.

Michael took me to his mother's house and told me, in great confidence, that John Mac was coming from Nimule to pick up Michael and his other sisters, and take them across the border to Kenya. This John Mac had also heard that his own brother was in Nattinger, and he would try to liberate him, too.

At the very least, I was convinced that Michael thought that my brother John was alive and coming to get us. I still did not completely believe, though, that it was a fact. Someone who was dead in the war was dead until you saw them alive with your own two eyes.

Then, one day, my brother John appeared. He was injured – with new scars and agitated, fissured skin, the result of an insect bite he'd suffered in Juba – but he was very much alive. He also wore officer's stripes.

For many years I had thought John had been killed in battle, and he had thought the same of me, so it was an emotional reunion. John was far more practised in affection than I, and he showed it more easily, but I know he could tell how happy I was at finding him alive.

John had official dispensation from the army to drive to Kakuma in Kenya to receive more medical treatment for his wounds, and to take Elizabeth's family with him – Michael, and Michael's mother and sisters. John was expected to return to the war, but he had no intention of doing that.

In the never-ending spider web of distrust that existed in the SPLA, friction between some elements of the ruling clique and the Dinka-Bor had emerged. John was a visible representative of the latter, and a lightning rod of distrust. John spoke some English, and was better educated than many of the SPLA men – having learned a little in the church at Mading near our village that the Arabs destroyed. Many of the uneducated officers in the SPLA were quick to draw assumptions about John's ambitions. In the SPLA, having ambition but without the guns to back it up was often a death sentence.

Although John – like most good officers – had a few things to say about the prosecution of the war, he was no dissenter or mutineer. Some months before we left, he had been treated as such, though. A small faction of powerful men, led by Dr John Garang's wayward son, Mabior Garang, had had John pulled from the front line, arrested without charge, interrogated and tortured. Eventually John was released, but at that point he knew that if he stayed in South Sudan, he would most likely not survive the war. Not only had he pushed the limits of luck in frontline engagements, but now he was also threatened from behind.

ABOVE LEFT: With my nephew, Joshua. Australia gave us both the chance at a new beginning.

ABOVE RIGHT: Like so many teens, music helped me feel connected. This a photo of me meeting American rapper Xzibit after a concert.

BELOW: I spent a lot of time on the soccer field of Blacktown Workers Club. If I wasn't studying, eating or sleeping, I was playing football.

ABOVE: My brother John, known to our Sudanese family as Mac. Thanks to John's tenacity and the kindness of Christine (*pictured here*) and Bob Harrison, we were accepted as refugees into Australia.

BELOW: John became very good friends with foreign correspondent Hugh Riminton (*right*). Hugh has kindly written the foreword to this book.

ABOVE: Here I am with some of my family in Australia: John's wife Elizabeth, my nephew Joshua, and my niece Guet.

BELOW: I was a young man who still carried the scars of war and the nightmares from battle, but I was lucky – I could see education was the key to breaking free of the war boy I had been.

ABOVE: Graduating from Western Sydney University was a huge moment in my life and it wouldn't have happened without John. I love this photo of us together at my graduation.

BELOW: Since that first degree, I have completed my Masters at the University of Wollongong and I am still studying today. I believe that education is freedom and is the key to helping the disenfranchised.

ABOVE: Being able to give a voice to refugees and the disenfranchised, and hope to new Australians about the possibilities that hard work and focus can bring is a gift and a privilege.

BELOW: I am very proud of the law practice I have set up with Joe Correy. The AC (Adut-Correy) Law Group has its offices in the Western Sydney suburb of Blacktown. The law is what I love.

ABOVE: I had no idea how the short film about my life, made by Western Sydney University, would be received. After over two million views on YouTube it has helped others understand the horrors that see people seek asylum in safer countries. For me, it has meant many opportunities to share my story and to promote the importance of education.

BELOW: Sitting for artist Nick Stathopoulos as he painted my portrait to enter into the Archibald Prize was just one of the amazing things that has happened to me since the film was made. It was an honour to watch Nick work and I was incredibly impressed by the finished painting. You can see it on the inside back cover of this book. (Photo supplied by Nick Stathopoulos)

ABOVE: In 2016, I returned to South Sudan. I met with Colonel Carey, who was based at the United Nations Mission in South Sudan (UNMISS) base.

BELOW: The saddest moment of my return was visiting my brother John's grave in Goi. I kneeled near a mound of dirt next to the school that John had built with such hope. That hope was extinguished in 2013. John's body lay under that mound and I took my shirt off and buried it in the dirt. It was all I had to give him that day.

Seeing my mother in her village was a bitter sweet moment. My mother would never cope with leaving her country. She wants to die there. But she still lectured me that I was too old and should be married by now (*top*). I know my mother is proud of me, and as long as she lives my heart will belong to both Australia and South Sudan. An Australian life goes on for me, a South Sudanese one for her. But knowing the danger she is in haunts me every day.

The day after our reunion, John explained to me how the Dinka-Bor had been treated by the SPLA, and that he was taking Elizabeth's family so he could resettle them somewhere safe in Africa. He also said that, with the help of his Christian god, he and Elizabeth would try to eventually get to a western country and live western lives, where they could live freely, prosperously and happily. I didn't really understand what living a western life was, and I really didn't understand what it was to prosper and live freely, but when John said that he wanted to take me with him, I was excited by his enthusiasm.

'You are young enough that you don't have to have a life that is only war. You could have a career if you wanted to, Deng. You're smart, and you work hard. You could still have an education.'

Since the moment back in our village when Adut had lied to me and told me I was going to get an education in Ethiopia, I had often thought about what an education might be. My real dream was of going back to the front line, though. I had no desire to leave the war, but I didn't want to leave John and his strange, unbridled positivity either. All of the other connections in my life had been severed; even those with Dr John Garang and my AK-47, because I had not been trained to guard tailors, mechanics and terrified Arabs.

Finding a brother again reminded me of how strong family bonds could be, and John, in particular, was such a dynamic influence.

John said the first stop in our journey would be the giant refugee camp Kakuma, in northern Kenya. I had actually thought of trying to make it to Kakuma before, when I was stuck as part of the *moakin*. A lot of boys from Nattinger had tried to escape to Kakuma, but from what I could tell, the success rate had been very low. Some had been killed on the way, but more had been returned by the SPLA, after having been severely beaten.

It was because of John's incandescent persuasiveness and family fealty that I agreed to go with him. With his stripes on his shoulder and confidence in his step, he walked into my barracks and ordered the commanding officer to allow me to travel to Lokichogio for further treatment for my wounds.

The officers at Nattinger would have no part of it. I'd been on unrestricted duties for months, and they'd seen me playing football most days. The request was not only refused, it most likely created a healthy amount of suspicion. John decided we would be leaving the next night. To stay longer would be dangerous for us both.

When the time came, I felt little of the drama of the moment. For me, it was just another moment of randomness in the story of my childhood. If we succeeded, I would just be in another camp, hungry and sick, yearning to be fighting. If we didn't make it, I would be beaten and sent back to the menial duties of Nattinger life, yearning to be fighting.

For John, though, this moment could mean a life free of war and poverty, not just for him, but for his wife. It could also mean death. John was an officer, so a seditious act such as the one he was suggesting would almost certainly mean capital punishment.

On the day of our escape, I considered backing out. Leaving in this way felt like I was avoiding the battlefield that I craved so badly. A hatred of cowardice had been drummed into my every cell, and escaping seemed like a coward's act. I wondered if I could ask the officers if I would ever be allowed to fight again and if the answer was no then I would leave. But I realised I couldn't do that. That would show my brother's hand. John was my older brother, and seniority had meant a lot to the boy who had once lived on the White Nile.

That night I was scheduled to have sentry duty from 8 p.m. to 4 a.m. We planned to flee the base at 3 a.m. I manned my station until my shift was close to being done before I quietly slipped back to the barracks. I tucked my AK-47 into my bed, bunched my blankets so it might look to an uninterested eye like I was still sleeping, and then I fled to Elizabeth's mother's house.

There I met John and the others, and we piled into a truck that John had arranged for us. At that point in the war both strategic allies and humanitarian benefactors were supplying much of the food that was being consumed by the SPLA, and many of the officers were taking the opportunity to sell that food in Kenya or Uganda to either buy more munitions, or line their pockets. The truck John had arranged was full of sacks of corn; sacks that were supposed to end up in South Sudanese mouths, but were destined for sale in Kenya.

As we left Nattinger, John and the members of Elizabeth's family – all holders of papers that allowed them to move freely towards Kenya – rode in the cabin of the truck. I, who was paperless, hid behind the sacks of corn.

It was a twelve-hour journey from Nattinger to Kakuma, and I spent all of it bouncing around, waiting for check-points, of which there were many. At each checkpoint the guards seemed uninterested in the truck and its contents – there was just some perfunctory conversation and then we were off again.

When we arrived in Lokichogio, we said goodbye to Elizabeth's family and wished them well (they were staying in Lokichogio) and then we started walking as briskly as we could manage south, away from the influence of the SPLA, and towards the mass of humanity that was Kakuma refugee camp.

The camp had been set up in 1991, primarily to support the flood of people fleeing the war in Sudan but by the time John and I got to Kakuma it was accommodating people fleeing at least six other wars. Virtually possession-less and penniless, the two of us walked to the intake area of the camp and, eventually, were registered as official refugees.

Then my official refugee life started, which was almost indiscernible from a great part of the life I'd lived as a soldier. There was more food in Kenya, but not much. There was some medicine, and it was greatly needed. There were no bombings, but there was very little hope.

We were taken to an area of Dinka-Bor refugees, and there we found Elizabeth, as well as people who had been there since the very beginning of the war. There was talk of some people being resettled in places like Canada and America, and even Australia, but it wasn't happening to the people around us. It only took a few weeks for all of us to yearn for a life other than the one we were living in Kakuma.

In the many dead, dusty days at Kakuma, I dreamed of being back in a fighting brigade, facing the guns of the Arabs: without my AK-47 I felt naked.

I asked John if he wanted to go back to the war. He said he didn't. He said we'd taken our first step towards a new life and all he was thinking about was the steps that would follow. He wasn't just looking out for me; he and Elizabeth were now expecting a child. I believed what he said, as every day he hustled and worked to get us out of Kakuma. Every day my brother was meeting people about how an application for external residency could become a reality. John used all the English he had learned when he was a Bible student to find out everything he could about the application for an international visa. There was no man or woman, black or white, he would not press to find out how we could get out of the camp. John also travelled out of the camp, often as far as the Kenyan capital, Nairobi, more than 700 kilometres south, where he would petition and apply and harangue to try to increase the likelihood of us being relocated.

John was away in Nairobi when his first son was born, and the boy was delivered into Elizabeth's arms, and mine. This would be a theme in John's life, and mine. Elizabeth named the boy Joshua but, as tribal law dictated, the name would not be permanent until John returned. When he did come back, John had no objection to the strong, western, Biblical name.

Shortly after meeting his son, John was back in Nairobi. While John hustled outside of the camp, I hustled inside, hunting around the camp for discarded tin cans in a decent condition, and then turning them into small stoves and selling them, so Elizabeth, Joshua and I could augment our daily rations.

When John came back from the capital, he had been unsuccessful, but he had even more resolve. He'd heard that our chances of relocation might be improved by moving over to one of the two enormous refugee camps, Dadaab and Ifo, closer to the Somali border.

It was a long and hungry journey to those two camps and, in both, we found more than 100,000 Somalis fleeing another many-headed civil war, which had started in the 1980s and was yet to end. There were Sudanese at both camps, but our numbers were small by comparison, and the militant Somali groups in the camp, who had no problems bringing their weapons into the supposedly demilitarised camps, hated us as only true believers can hate apostates.

There was gunfire most nights in those camps. When I heard the snap of the bullets, it would anger me greatly as I thought about the pointless waste of potentially dying in a war that wasn't even mine. The gunfire usually came from a group called Al-Shifta, which would later become internationally famous as Al-Shabaab – one of the most violent actors in one of the most brutal theatres of war in the world.

Al-Shifta would sometimes sweep through the Sudanese part of those camps, firing in the air and asserting their dominance. The role of us Sudanese in that particular charade was to flee.

One night in the Ifo camp, when the guns started to rattle, and my countrymen and women started to run, I decided that if the Al-Shifta wished to kill me, then I would let them. I would not be running anymore.

I lay in my cot as the Islamists swept through the camp, and I waited for a bullet. No Al-Shifta men came into my tent that night, though. They just rolled past me, like an unbroken wave.

When the Al-Shifta men disappeared, John returned and then he and I had the worst of our many arguments. He told me I had lost my memory of what a life was worth, and I told him he had lost his memory of what pride was. He told me I was an idiot, and I told him he was a coward. After that last word, John went into a rage and beat me very badly, lacerating and bruising my face and body. It was the first and last time he ever beat me, but he got his money's worth.

It's common for Sudanese parents and older siblings to beat young children when they get out of line, but I wouldn't accept a beating from John. I was a soldier, not some child. Yes, he was my older brother, but I was not well practised at being a younger brother, or a family member at all. It had been so long. The beating didn't just anger me, it confused me and I simply couldn't accept it.

After the beating John left in some distress himself. After I washed the blood away from my face, I went to one of the holes in the camp fence and walked into the dark. I was hundreds and hundreds of kilometres from the South Sudanese border, but my vague goal was to make it there. Perhaps I would stop when I got to Kakuma, but I didn't know. I just wanted to be away from John.

After four or five hours walking, I was spotted by relatives and taken back to the camp. When John and I were reunited there was no real reconciliation. I long harboured real hatred for him after he beat me, but an acceptance came, born through necessity. We were stuck together, for the time being.

Eventually John reconciled with the fact that we were unlikely to be found to be international refugees in the eastern camps, so he decided that if we were to be stuck in a purgatory, we might as well be with our countrymen. It took us several weeks to return to the Dinka-Bor part of Kakuma, which had been square one of our refugee journey.

I don't know how, but John still managed to maintain hope and every day he forced me to learn new English words and phrases, which he insisted I would need in my new country.

'Good morning.'

'Thank you very much.'

'Nice to meet you.'

'It is a lovely day.'

I took it all on board while my boring Kakuma life continued. John, for his part, never ceased in his efforts to find a way out. There was no person John wouldn't bail up about processing or sponsoring, no lead he wouldn't chase to the very end, no matter how weak it was.

John told me little about his efforts to get us resettled, probably because I never asked. I didn't really care much about moving. Here, there, in Kenya, in Canada – none of it meant enough to me for me to ask about it.

Then John met a *kawaja* woman, a counsellor from Australia who was trying to help people in the camp with their bad dreams and sad faces. The woman, who said she wasn't helping as much as she had hoped, was a Christian, like John, and they would have long conversations about God, the war and Australia.

John became very excited when he heard that this woman, whose name was Christine Harrison, had decided to help one of the people in the camp leave the camp life we were half-living.

'I can't spend all of this time here and not help at least one of you,' she had said to John. That was what Christine had decided, she would save one person from the camp, and help them resettle in Australia.

John had heard that Christine was married, so he assumed he would have to get the approval of Christine's husband before she could do anything. He asked Christine for her husband's phone number. With that number in hand, John set off to the only place where he knew he could make a phone call, Nairobi, 700 kilometres away.

John must have believed strongly in this lead because, before he left, he made me promise that I would sneak into the organised English classes for refugees who were on the verge of emigration.

John had taught me those few English phrases and I already had a jumble of languages in my head – Arabic, Amharic, Dinka, Nuer – but I often didn't know the source of the words I was using. When I started those classes, I was happy to find that a lot of the words I had been using in my country were actually from the English language.

I enjoyed learning what English words I could, but just for the joy of learning not because I thought much about their application, like John did. I had little conception of the life that the people who were moving on after their English lessons were to be living. John talked about America and Australia, but those places meant little to me, except that I had enjoyed the *digigstralia* so much.

I was still, in my mind, a soldier. My mind could not escape the war nor, did it seem, could John's body.

It took some weeks for John to return from making that phone call, and when he came back he had fresh injuries, including a broken skull. John had had the extreme misfortune to be in the Kenyan capital at the same time as some of his factional rivals from the SPLA, including Dr John Garang's son Mabior.

John was grabbed off the street, blindfolded and taken to a house in the outer suburbs of Nairobi. There, Mabior and his friends tortured him, and beat him until his skull cracked open. Unconscious and bleeding, John was assumed to be dead, so they dumped his lifeless body into a rubbish bin.

When he came to, John dragged himself to a clinic and was treated. After that, the Kenyan police came to take him to jail, as they were in the pocket of the SPLA and wanted to see if Mabior wished to finish the job. John was released after a week. When he returned to us in Kakuma, many days later, he was a broken and battered man. He had knife slashes, blunt-force trauma wounds, and bruises all over his body.

Though physically broken, John was ebullient. He had spoken to Christine's husband, Bob, and even though Bob had not heard of his wife's plans to help a refugee, he said he would get the wheels in motion for us to gain Australian visas.

Despite John's words of hope, I saw his new wounds and I became even more convinced that the war would never end for us. That was neither a depressing thought nor an exhilarating thought, it was just a soldier's thought. I felt deathly hatred for the men who had tortured and conspired to kill my brother. I can still feel it now. It's the kind of hatred that has kept my country in a state of conflict and misery for decades, but even in my position of privilege, I find it hard to generate the forgiveness or even self-interest required to mitigate the hatred I feel. They do not deserve forgiveness. I try to not feel hatred, but I still desperately wish for justice for those who hurt John.

Bob and Christine were true to their word. For us to be relocated, they would need to guarantee John accommodation, a job and the price of a flight to Sydney for him and his dependants. With the help of their church, they managed to fulfil all of those requirements. A little less than six months after John had returned from Nairobi, we were being told to head south to the capital, where we would be given Australian visas.

I tried to share John and Elizabeth's excitement. I tried, but I couldn't. Perhaps it was a fear of change that I had developed the day I was taken from my mother, perhaps it was because there was too much war still in my blood – I don't know what it was, but I felt nothing while John and Elizabeth were vibrating with happiness.

We were relocated temporarily to Nairobi, and I had never seen such a place, with more cars on the road than I had ever seen cows in a field. There was so much food too – all types of meat and fruit and vegetables and milk. It seemed that there was no need to be hungry in Nairobi.

But we were not welcome in Nairobi, even though we were there legally.

Nearly every time we went outside, the police stopped us, and even when we showed them our visas and exit papers, they still threatened to lock us up and take our accreditation unless we greased their palms.

John was scared that he would be thrown into jail, and possibly sent back across the border, but in each instance the cops were just shaking us down. We were the poorest citizens of perhaps the poorest country on earth, but the Nairobi police still wished to squeeze us if they could. We kept a very low profile before our flight.

The day before we left for Australia, a cousin of ours whom I had heard of as he ascended through the SPLA ranks, visited us. His name was Makuei Deng, and he had risen to the rank of general, but even that elevated rank had not kept him immune from the internal friction that perpetually plagued the SPLA. General Makuei had also suffered torture at the hands of the SPLA, and was in Nairobi receiving treatment for various wounds.

When John explained to the general where we would be resettling, Makuei told me I must be prepared for cold like I had never experienced before. I, like most of my people, hate the cold, and seeing the trepidation in my face, the general produced a gift.

'The cold is only to be feared when equipped with the wrong clothes. Take this,' he said, handing over a woollen vest.

On that day I was fourteen years of age, and I am still quite partial to adding a vest to my suits.

Chapter Seven

WELCOME TO AUSTRALIA

Even though the war in Sudan had been raging for years, we were only the third Sudanese family to come to Australia as refugees.

We flew to Sydney with Cathay Pacific, and I hated every moment of it. From Nairobi to Hong Kong the drone of the engine noise drove me mad, and we were hungry throughout the flight as we never figured out how to eat the plastic-covered food that was brought to us, and we were too timid to ask any questions of the flight attendants.

When we got to Hong Kong, we were delivered to a transit lounge, and there we sat in silence while Asian people stared and whispered. We were too scared to even speak to each other. I'd never met an Asian person before, and knew nothing about them. What did they want from us? Should I be scared of them? It was all too confusing to fathom.

The flight to Sydney was similarly unbearable, and we were not able to figure out how to eat the food on that leg either. Then we landed in Australia – a place that was as strange to me as Neptune may be to you.

There were giant illuminated signs, and everything was clean. A lot of people were frowning and everybody looked exactly the same, except for a very large, round man with a grey beard who was waiting for us when we emerged from customs.

This was Bob, the man who John had travelled more than 700 kilometres to speak to on the phone, and who, with his wife, had changed the trajectories of our lives. Bob had a smile that poured out of his beard and woollen jumpers for all of us in his hands. John was very happy when he saw this man and they hugged warmly.

As we walked out of the airport doors, I was hit with a cold I had never before felt and rushed to get my jumper over my body, tucking my hands up against my stomach.

John asked Bob where we were going now, and Bob told him we were going to a place called Blacktown. John's face sank as though he had just spied an SPLA roadblock.

Blacktown was surely the Kakuma of Sydney – a dusty, sparse ghetto where all of the arriving black people would be dumped.

John eventually asked Bob how long we would have to stay in Blacktown, and Bob said we'd be there for a few days, to set ourselves up, and then we could visit him in the Blue Mountains. That sounded much nicer.

Bob said he liked Blacktown, and that we'd probably like it there.

After leaving the airport he drove us straight to a restaurant called McDonald's, which was a palace of confusion. There were tables of wood that weren't made of wood, and people dressed up in uniforms who weren't soldiers, and there were huge pictures of food pasted on the walls, only I couldn't see where the food actually was.

John said that Bob would arrange for the food to be brought to us. Bob spoke to one of the people in uniform and, after a short while, food was brought out on trays.

I had a hamburger – I don't remember which one – and it was perhaps the strangest thing I had ever eaten. I was hungry though, so I wolfed it down along with the yellow potato strings that accompanied it. When we finished our meal, Bob drove us to this Blacktown, which was absolutely nothing like Kakuma.

Bob worked for a charity called Marist Youth Care, and he had arranged an apartment for us above their offices, which had previously been a convent adjacent to a school and church. It was a small, two-bedroom place, but for us it was a palace, filled with technological wonders and food the likes of which we hadn't even known existed. After the long journey to Australia, I laid my body down on the first real bed I'd ever seen, under my first duvet, and I slept in a country at peace.

I will, for the rest of my life, be grateful to the people and organisations of Western Sydney for welcoming me into their fold, and I am proud that, as you read this sentence, I am most likely at my desk in my office, reading depositions, just a short distance away from that apartment. I especially appreciate everything the Marists did for us – from flying us over, to arranging a job for John as the caretaker of the grounds surrounding our apartment. Things were not easy in those early days, though.

Everything from crossing the road to heating the oven (Elizabeth tried to heat it with kindling and fire) was confusing to us, and the Marists were our only tether to sense. After a couple of days in Blacktown, Bob was true to his word and took us to his and Christine's house in the Blue Mountains, where we met their family.

Bob and Christine took us for a walk into the bush, and my heart filled when I saw rock formations that looked like home. Even though the rocks and mountains looked more like Eastern Equatoria (especially Nattinger) I started to think about the Nile, and my village.

I thought briefly about my mother. It had been almost a decade since I'd seen her, and I wondered what she looked like, if she was even alive. Even now it's almost impossible to get information from the villages, let alone then, while the war was still raging. I had trouble remembering her face, or a situation I could place her in. It no longer felt like a real place, my village, nor did this new place with its yellow string potatoes, and the white people who all looked like one another. Even the war had started to stop feeling real, and that made me sad. I felt untethered.

Although I had a general sense of unease, a good part of that day in the bush was actually quite nice. John, Elizabeth and Joshua were happy, and the sun was shining, which felt good on my skin, and Bob was so kind and friendly. When the sun went down though, and the winter air started to chill, any happiness left me. There is no summer or winter in the south of Sudan, there is only the hot wet and the hot dry. The first real winter night I'd ever experienced was in the Blue Mountains, and it was a freezing one.

I was unaccustomed to being inside a building, but in the Blue Mountains I couldn't go outside either, because when I did my skin would feel like it was starting to burn. I had never in my life been cold before, let alone that cold.

When I woke and rose, it was possibly even colder than when I'd gone to bed. There was frost underfoot and, as I walked around Bob's yard, it crunched. I had never seen ice before, and I hated it. The cold was my enemy. I hated the way it stopped my mouth from working, and turned my breath into smoke; it was all so unnatural.

That morning if I could have clicked my fingers and been transported back to Kakuma, or even Nattinger, I would have done it without a thought. I told John how I felt. He was angry, as I knew he would be, but also compassionate, as I knew he would be. After all, the cold was a shock to him too.

The next day, John and I tried to register with Centrelink – the Australian social security service – and we found that they were not well set up for African refugees.

As a minor, I would need a legal guardian in Australia, which was a strange concept for me because the closest I'd had to a guardian since the age of seven were superior officers from the SPLA. For my brother to be my guardian, he and I had to have the same surname, or at least a good reason why we didn't. Dinka-Bor naming convention was apparently not a good reason.

John's full name was John Mac Acuek, so for us to register with the refugee papers that we had been given in Kenya, I had to take on John's surname. When I was given my Centrelink accreditation, I found a name on the form that meant absolutely nothing to me and bore no similarity to the names my family gave me, nor any mention of my clan's history.

When we got back to the apartment, I voiced forcefully my displeasure in having to change my name. John was ever the pragmatist, though.

'Who cares what those people call you? You will always be Deng.'

'But this is not my name. This is nobody's name and it means nothing,' I told John holding up my Centrelink ID bearing the name 'Dave Machacuek'.

'If Dave Machacuek gets to eat food and go to school, then I would want to be him.'

Just a few days later, Dave Machacuek was enrolled to be a student at Evans High School. I turned up that freezing morning at the high school confused, and suffered silently through Literature, Mathematics and Human Biology classes.

I spoke to no students, understood nothing that the teachers said, and yearned for the day to end. I was fifteen then, and that was the first day of traditional schooling I had ever done. It was not what I'd expected.

When I got home I told John I could not do another day like that. I told my brother I would have rather been tortured than sit in those classes while the white people stared and the teachers droned on in what to me sounded like gibberish. I told John I was still angry at being called Dave too, and would no longer answer to that name. John knew I was adamant – this was not just teenage discontent.

John could be a hard man, but he did not lack compassion either. He told me he would make sure that I could change my name back, and he realised that they were not going to teach me what I really needed to learn at Evans High School. At Evans High School they were decorating rooms, but I still needed to build the foundation. I needed to learn English.

I didn't go back to Evans High School. I didn't want to go outside at all, really. I didn't even know how to cross the road, and I would get looks everywhere I went, so I spent most of the first couple of weeks in Australia sitting on the floor with Joshua watching a television show (a rare luxury in Kakuma) with four men wearing skivvies and singing simple, catchy songs.

It turned out I didn't have to leave the house to get myself into trouble, though. When we first got to the apartment one of the Marists explained how everything therein worked. When they got to the microwave they explained it to John and me as 'a box that heats food up'. Like a fire, right? I understood that.

The Marists delivered some groceries for us, including cans of Coca-Cola which they put in the fridge. I decided that I'd have one of the cans. Having never had a cold drink before, I decided to warm the can up in the box that heats up food.

The can exploded in the microwave, of course, but not before creating a terrifying, localised electrical storm of lightning and sound that I thought would destroy the apartment. I was scared of the microwave after that, and felt like an idiot, until Elizabeth did the exact same thing a couple of weeks later.

After a few idle weeks of staying in the apartment and playing with Josh, John arranged for me to start on an intensive English course at Blacktown TAFE.

That first day at TAFE was really my first day as a student. When I sat down in class I was confused, because I thought all of the people were white and I had assumed that all white people were able to speak English. It turned out that not all white people could speak English, and also that a lot of the people in that class were not white at all but were Indian or South East Asian. They had all looked like *kawaja* to me.

Most of the people at the course were as lacking in English language skills as I was, so I had finally found a place in Australia that didn't confuse me. A place where I fitted in. We were all learning together, like all of us boys getting our military training in Nattinger.

As I managed to get a pencilled hand around my first English letters, and my mouth around some single-syllabled words, I started to feel achievement. I would think often about being back in my village when Adut the stammerer told me I had to go to Ethiopia to get an education. Now, ten or so years later, I was actually getting an education. It felt good.

I would study every night with John, showing him my workbooks and getting him to elaborate on my answers, and place the words I had learned into a context I understood. I pretended as though my TAFE work was a chore, but the truth was it was the one thing I was enjoying in Australia. I would never tell John that, though. I thought he was trying to make me a soft family man and, for some reason, I felt like I needed to keep the edge I'd gotten as a soldier. I don't know why. I think a part of me was still harbouring the possibility of getting my AK-47 back, and getting involved in the war again.

The war was still deep inside of me. I barely slept when I got to Australia, because when I did sleep, I would have vivid and dynamic Sudanese nightmares. Sometimes I would be back assaulting Kapoeta, or running from the bombs, but often the nightmares would be less literal, with me being pursued by something that I couldn't quite discern, or manically running to find something that I'd lost. The two themes in my nightmares were running, and an electric fear of something worse than death. Often I would wake up somewhere other than my bed, having run into a wall or some furniture.

My insomnia would spur me to ask for more and more TAFE work. During the day it was easier to fill my head with television and school, and play with my nephew, but at night, in the dark, my head would only go to the bad places – places that were only slightly better than the places I went to when I was asleep.

On Sundays John would make me go to church with Bob and Elizabeth but I wasn't one for sitting down for long periods of time, while being lectured in a language I didn't understand. The people there were very nice and welcoming though, and I made my first Australian friend there.

That man's name was Geoff Hicherson, a large, retired police detective, who used to work out of Blacktown Local Area Command. The first time I went to church, Geoff bounded up to us, introduced himself and his family – Geoff had two sons, Paul and Ian, who were roughly the same age as me, and a wife, Margaret, just as kind as he – and started talking to me. Even though I couldn't understand a word he was saying, the smiles and greetings spoke a universal language of kindness. I loved being in Geoff's presence.

Partly through mime, partly through broken English, Geoff asked me what kind of things I liked to do, and I told him that I liked to play soccer. Geoff grabbed that information with both hands, arranging for me to start football training with his son, Paul. He would pick me up from the apartment before training, and drop me off as well. And, more often than not, he would arrange a meal afterwards that my stomach would be able to handle, and he did it all wholly through the kindness of his heart.

The war I'd left seemed like such a large thing, and the charity of a churchman and his football-playing son a small thing by comparison, but Geoff's kindness was an integral part of my integration into Australian society.

There are few things in this world that are genuinely ubiquitous, but it's true of football. While I understood almost no aspects of Australian life, I understood the goals and the ball, and the offside rule and the joy of scoring, in the exact same way every Australian player did.

Paul was an excellent soccer player. When I started training with him I had a game that had some raw usefulness but little polish. I was very fast, though, and fit, and soon, I was training with Paul's excellent club side, the Fairfield Bulls.

Our coach was a man named Marshall Soper, a former Socceroos player, whose strict discipline and impressive expertise reminded me of Commander Majok. Training under Marshall was exactly what I needed in my life. He was an Australian man whom I respected, and didn't want to disappoint. That football training was a nice midpoint between military life and Australian life, and each session put a little bit more purpose into my life.

After I started playing football, my TAFE English studies went from strength to strength. I'd do all of my homework quite quickly, and then augment it with long hours of lying on the lounge room floor with little Joshua, watching the Wiggles. The Wiggles were of particular use for me. The slow cadence of their speech, and the comic exaggeration they used helped me contextualise all the words they were using. Sometimes I found myself watching Josh's Wiggles DVDs without him.

At football training, players would sometimes catch me singing 'Big Red Car' or 'Hot Potato, Hot Potato' to myself and laugh. It was embarrassing but I didn't care. Apart from football, the only thing I really cared about then was learning English.

In retrospect, I should have cared more about the dedication and sacrifices that John had made. He had a plan, for me, for Elizabeth and for Joshua, but the fierce sense of independence that had been instilled in me over the war years made it difficult for me to respect John the way I should have. I should have cared more about John and Elizabeth, but I didn't let myself. I wouldn't let myself become soft and caring.

I didn't yet value how good life was in Australia – too much of the war was still in me, too much of the death wish. I found it hard to give thanks to John for taking me away from East Africa and I'm sure a therapist worth their salt would suggest that I feared the attachment of family lest they judge or disappear.

If I'd recognised that, perhaps I might have recognised how difficult John was finding life in Australia. Instead, I saw him as a fixed position – the confident and driven man I'd known back in Sudan. John and I bickered sometimes, we argued other times and, on rare occasions, we fought bitterly. On those occasions, Geoff and Margaret welcomed me into their house, giving me a meal and a bed for the night. Geoff was an excellent, patient teacher and from him I learned a lot about language, and the Australian way of life.

When I was at home, I would consume the English language like fire does a dry tree. I'd sometimes do my TAFE homework two or three times, and after that I would read passages from the Bible, and then recite them in long, fast, rote strings, like a chant. I would stay awake as long as I could, mumbling those passages to myself, trying to stave off the nightmares.

I thought the nightmares would become more infrequent the longer I was in Australia, but that wasn't the case. Soon I managed to make my days so full I barely thought about Sudan, but at night I couldn't help but think about bombs and guns and dead bodies. Especially when I fell asleep.

The church people suggested I try counselling, and I did try one session, but very quickly I surmised that they couldn't do anything for me. I wasn't really ready to speak, nor was the counsellor I spoke to equipped to help me with the kinds of things that I had done and seen. I knew it would be strong men like Geoff, Bob and Marshall who were going to help assimilate me into modern life, not well-intentioned, but painfully under-prepared therapists.

I remember an instance at one of those early church visits when Geoff gave me a twenty-dollar note. I asked what it was for, and he explained that the money was to go into my back pocket, not for fun or food, but for an occasion when it was actually needed. He said I would know that moment when it arrived.

That occasion would come just a couple of weeks later when I was attempting to catch the train for the first time. I had never seen a train before, let alone caught one, so I walked into Blacktown station, as confused as a puppy in a thunderstorm. I didn't really understand about timetables and tickets and routes.

After some time I figured out which train I wanted to take, and when it was arriving. When the doors opened, I jumped on board without solving the ticket conundrum. A few stations later, some ticket inspectors stopped me.

When they started asking questions I couldn't understand, I started to think that perhaps they would take me to jail or that they may even send me back to Sudan. Eventually I got them to call Geoff, and he explained my situation. When we got off, they showed me how to buy a ticket, which I did with the twenty dollars Geoff had given me. Since then I have always paid for whatever I am supposed to pay for.

That moment felt like a cultural breakthrough. I wasn't admonished or beaten by the ticket inspectors who found me, I was helped, and I was proud when I managed to purchase my first train ticket. Baby steps, baby steps.

The problem was, for every conundrum I solved, I found another. Even as my English improved quickly, everything about Australian life was still so confusing, from buying food in a supermarket to crossing a busy intersection.

For the first few months in Australia, I lived a very cloistered life. The paths I took to TAFE or my apartment, or to Geoff's, or to the fields where I played football were always the same because, on the routes I took, people expected me. Blacktown is now quite flush with Sudanese people, but back then seeing a boy of such dark skin was a novelty. I had been background noise in South Sudan, and I hated the surprise I saw in people's faces in Sydney.

When I walked on the footpath, it felt like everyone stared, and pointed and whispered. I was ill prepared to be an anomaly. It was especially hard for me when I had to go into businesses owned by Arabic people, who I'd been taught my whole life were killers and the enemy. I'd feel their eyes burning into me with their stares.

As far as I knew, there were only two other African families in Sydney then, a North Sudanese family who we had little in common with, and a Dinka family from the state of Bahr el Ghazal, who used to visit our apartment from time to time. Due to the rules of seniority, and because they had no children my age, it was really only John who spent time talking with that family.

Then, one day I saw an African guy walking down the street in Blacktown. I cut across the road, and intercepted him.

'Deng Adut,' I said, putting my hand out.

'Lamin Colley,' he replied, not at all taken aback by me being so forward.

That was it – we were mates, and I have been close to Lamin from that day on.

Lamin worked at Woolworths full time, and had his own apartment, so soon I spent more time with him than with John, Elizabeth and Josh. Lamin and I usually watched the English Premier League, and he helped me with my English homework.

My English was too limited for us to actually hold a conversation, but we appreciated each other's company enough that it didn't matter. We often used to speak to each other in gibberish – a mishmash of real words in many languages, and made-up sounds – just to feel as though we were speaking like friends would. I used to devour those conversations of nonsense. I'd forgotten what it was like to have a contemporary.

Over the next few weeks and months, we started to accumulate – usually at soccer matches – more and more disenfranchised African teenagers. There was Mickeyas, an Ethiopian; Aji, a Ghanian; Joseph and Robert Awalla, two South Sudanese brothers; and another South Sudanese teen named Richard Aconda, who'd been in Australia since the 1980s. We are all still friends today.

Lamin's apartment almost ended up serving as a drop-in centre for the African youth of Blacktown, and we spent hour upon hour there, enjoying the company of people who understood us.

Richard especially was a huge help for me. Not only was his English first class, he also spoke Juba Arabic, a language I'd picked up a lot of during the war. My English improved in leaps and bounds at that time, and having a place where I felt accepted also helped me emotionally.

There was only one place we spent more time at than Lamin's apartment and that was the soccer field at Blacktown Workers Club. If I wasn't sleeping, or eating or studying, I was playing football at that field.

At first we played every day until sunset, but after we found the switch that turned on the floodlights we played deep into the night. When we could literally play no more, we would head back to Lamin's apartment for a barbecue feast and long, involved discussions about the intricacies of the English language. Those African boys became the bedrock of my Australian life.

People like Geoff and Bob were a godsend, but at some point you need contemporaries who understand your struggle because they are experiencing it too. Those boys were my African island, and my first real comfort in Australia.

But I knew that eventually I would have to swim out into the difficult waters away from that comfortable place if I was to make a life in Australia. All of us African boys knew that. We would need to make Australian friends, work in Australian workplaces, and have relationships with Australian women.

My first relationship with an Australian girl was with a friend of a friend. Alison was lovely and compassionate, and she gave me faith that I would someday be able to articulate myself properly. At that stage my English was still elementary but Ali seemed to understand everything I was trying to tell her. The connection that we had was legitimate, and I started to believe that I could fit in. I wasn't a novelty to her, I was a person and I loved her for that.

Our relationship was intense, as most relationships are at that age, and that intensity peaked when Ali and I had a pregnancy scare.

My initial reaction to this news was relief. When I'd been shot through the testicles, it wasn't a western doctor who'd treated me, but a rushed soldier doing combat triage. I had no idea if I would ever be able to get a woman pregnant. For any young man, that would be a concern, but for a Dinka teenager who had questioned the status of his manhood for some years, it was doubly so.

In English 'to have balls' means to have masculine power, but in Dinka culture testicles are not just the figurative centre of manhood, they are the defining characteristic. After a certain age, there are no respectable Dinka men without children.

In a situation where I should have been thinking of what Alison needed, I was only thinking of myself.

Ali and I were just teenagers, and both still in school, so I was ill equipped to understand the emotional experience it would be for Alison if she was pregnant. I can't imagine how hard it would have been for an Australian girl to be with me at that time, and to go through that ordeal. It all turned out okay but the relationship didn't last; it started to disintegrate after the pregnancy, but I'm still friendly with Ali to this day and only think of her fondly. She was and is a compassionate person, and I only wish I could have been more compassionate myself when she needed me to be.

At the time, though, I was confused and angered by the dissolution of that relationship, and I convinced myself that my lack of English was the primary issue, and not only that, I was sure that my ongoing confusion about Australian life was because of my language issues.

I redoubled my language efforts, spending every moment with an English speaker, or with a book in my hand. I found that picking up English words was not difficult, but turning them into sentences – into concepts and sense – took all of my concentration and patience, neither of which were traits I had brought with me to Australia.

Learning English wasn't an impossible task, however, just a very difficult one, and thankfully I had the help that I needed. I had my African friends, I had Josh and the Wiggles, and I had Geoff, who would drive all of us African misfits to our football games, while grilling me about verbs, nouns and adjectives.

If I had had an Australian godfather, it would have been Geoff. He took on the duties of a parent when a parent could not fulfil those duties, and he also led me to Christianity, a faith I dipped my toe into, but never fully immersed myself.

Although I really liked the morality and narratives of the Bible stories I read at night, I could never see them as anything more than just stories. As it had been in my village when John used to tell me about Christianity's big god, and his son Jesus, he felt it, but it never felt real to me.

John was devout, and you may imagine that his attachment to the church helped him integrate into Australian society, but it didn't. For all of us it was hard, but for him it was a particular shock. I don't know exactly the source of his discontent, but I think it was a mix of John losing the status that he had had in South Sudanese society, the general culture shock, and the struggle that he had with the English language. He came to Australia with a decent grasp of the language, but to start the university degree he wished to obtain, he realised he would need a much greater knowledge of the language than the passable English that he had.

Another reason that John couldn't comfortably live in Australia was because of Elizabeth. I don't know if their relationship issues were a by-product of the other stresses in their lives, or a multiplier of those issues, but they fought relentlessly almost from the day we got to Australia.

I think the tension between them was partly the result of a schism between what the marital expectations are for the Dinka, and what they are in Australia. I don't think either of them thought that their marriage should be wholly an Australian or Dinka union, but I also don't think they could ever agree where in the middle they should meet.

John took all the measures he could to make life better for his family in those early years, though. He took on his own TAFE course – that would not only teach him English, but potentially give him a tertiary entrance qualification – while also diligently fulfilling his caretaker position. But even when he was a student and a worker, he never really managed to feel comfortable in Australia, and he always talked about what life would be like when he had a good job, and money flowing.

When he finished his TAFE course, John quickly directed his attention to a university degree. John had always had a very rigid understanding of how the ladder of success in places like Australia was constructed and, as far as he was concerned, the first few rungs were educational.

John was accepted to study Social Science at Western Sydney University. We were delighted for him, but not surprised. When John saw a path, he would move heaven and earth to make sure he could walk it.

The path John saw for himself involved working on large international aid projects. He saw a middle-class dream in his future, but he would also never forget the African nightmare of his past. He couldn't forget how easily and cheaply lives could be improved in Sudan, and he wanted to be in a position to do just that, only not in Sudan – never in Sudan, and preferably not in Africa. John had always thought Africa would kill him if he returned.

When news about the war in Sudan was available (often it wasn't as it was a war that the west largely ignored, despite its enormous loss of life) I'd barely pay attention. John, however, and his friends – the Sudanese refugee population in Australia was starting to grow – would endlessly chew, like cow's cud, information about the fighting and potential treaties and political machinations.

John spoke of the war differently from the rest of the men, however. He didn't speak as though it was happening directly out the front of his door. John was always concerned about his family in South Sudan, and our tribe, but he was only attentive to the SPLA plight as their fortunes related to the people he loved.

For my part, those stories of treaties and alliances and international pressure meant almost nothing. I had never seen the war from the perspective of the eagle, I had only ever seen it through the eyes of the warthog. The war for me had only ever been visceral – never intellectual – and I was still largely divorced from my tribe and African family – the SPLA had seen to that.

When Australian troops landed in East Timor in 1999 after the UN ordered an intervention, John started dreaming of working in what would soon be the world's newest nation. The similarities between East Timor and the southern Sudanese struggle were striking, from the yoke of oppressive Islamic hegemons, to the questions of how a guerilla force could become a legitimate government.

First, however, he needed to complete his studies. John worked hard at university, but there were times when academic protocol confused him. I remember one instance when John submitted a major assignment about Dinka rituals for an anthropology class, only to be told he would have to cite his sources.

That confused John. He had lived what he was writing about, but his tutor had told him his information would be discounted unless some old *kawaja* author corroborated it. Those were the rules of the game though, so John reached out to his friend Hugh Riminton – an Australian journalist who had been welcomed by the Sudanese community after his excellent reporting of the war. Hugh found the book John needed in a Paddington second-hand bookstore.

During his degree, John was offered a scholarship to study at the University of Geneva and, with Riminton's help, he managed to take up the offer. John was overseas when Elizabeth gave birth to their second child, a girl. For that child John chose a very Sudanese name – Guet. It was the same name as one of our sisters. Once again, I was the first man to hold John's baby after she was born.

I didn't really understand why John wanted to be away; I always thought he should have been home with his children. I knew far less about parenting than most, but I knew what it was to grow up without the love and care of my parents. John did too – he'd left for the army when he was only a few years older than me – so his decision to be often absent confused and angered me.

In 2001 there was another sharp improvement in my English abilities, and that was the year I became confident conversing with strangers in English. I started to feel like I'd managed to tap into what I had previously seen as the beguiling but impenetrable magic that was regular Australian life.

The charms of a western life were starting to reveal themselves. My mind would still go back to Africa in my nightmares, but when I was awake I was concerned only with the English Premier League standings, or when my mates were going to be heading to Lamin's place, or what English homework I still had to do.

Around that time I got my first job, which was arranged by Geoff. It was a lawn-mowing gig at a large house in Minchinbury, and my efforts paid me twenty dollars at first, then twenty-five, and finally thirty, with my price having been renegotiated due to the extreme care I took in the presentation of that garden. Later that year I did some modelling too, signing up with a multi-ethnic modelling agency called 'Seven Flavours', which helped me put a lot more than twenty dollars in my pocket, and brought an African splash to advertisements for companies like KFC and Panasonic.

Then, again with the help of Geoff, I got a job at a petrol station in Blacktown. As he drove me to the interview, Geoff explained to me that this would be the perfect job for me. Not only would it help with my conversational English, I could do all my shifts at night, if I so chose. Geoff knew that I slept very little, due to my ongoing nightmares. I landed the job and Geoff bought me a second-hand push-bike so I could get to and from the petrol station.

The job did improve my English as I worked more and more shifts, but it also gave me more of an understanding of the complexity of Australian society. For the most part, people were respectful and friendly, but there were some people who were as furious and aggressive as some of the angrier soldiers I had met in Sudan.

Once, while at work, I watched a motorcyclist try to douse another man with petrol during a heated argument. Both had expensive-looking vehicles, and I couldn't stop wondering why people so rich would ever bother trying to kill each other.

I was robbed one night at work too. A gun was thrust in my face – not something I'd ever expected to have happen to me in Australia. It was quite late – maybe 2 or 3 a.m. – and a drug addict wearing a hoodie busted into the station with a handgun and threatened me. He wanted the money from the till in front of me, which I gave to him. Then he wanted more money. He grabbed my tie, pointed the gun at my belly, and then screamed for me to get him the money from the second till.

In my experience, if you point a weapon at someone, you're getting ready to commit murder, so I was convinced that this man was set to kill me once he had his money.

The second till was heavy with coins, and when the man motioned for me to dump the coins into a cradle he'd made with both his hands in his hoodie, I decided I would grab the gun after dumping the heavy coins into his shirt, and shoot him dead. Then I looked hard at the handgun and saw that it wasn't even loaded. This man was committing a robbery with an unloaded gun. He was an idiot. What if I had a gun? I certainly would have killed him.

I had no interest in a fistfight with a junkie over someone else's money, so I gave the man his meagre spoils and let him leave.

The man left with less than three hundred dollars. I didn't understand why anyone would find themselves in so desperate a spot when living in a place like Australia. With a very small amount of effort, one could be paid nearly three hundred dollars every day, without potentially being killed in the process. It made no sense to me.

After that incident with the junkie, life went on normally for me but for Cheryl, the shift manager, who had been in the back during the whole encounter, her mood had been permanently changed. She never came back to work, and I heard that she started having nightmares about that night. All that over three hundred dollars in small notes and change.

It was during that period while I was working at the petrol station that I also first experienced the sharp sting of overt, pointed racism. As many of the other African boys also worked at night and on weekends, our days off would often end up being during the week, and in spring and summer, we'd pile into a car or two and make the trek to Bondi Beach.

One day we parked a few streets away from the beach, and as we walked to the sand an older, white Australian man took it upon himself to start yelling at us.

'Oi, oi, fuckin' go get a job,' he yelled at us.

We all had jobs. We ignored him.

'Go get a job, go get a job, go get a job,' he yelled, as though it was a mantra.

'Just ignore him,' Mickeyas said. He was often our voice of reason.

Our refusal to engage with this man only angered him, though.

'Fuckin' lazy niggers,' he spat.

Niggers. The word didn't quite have the inherent power to hurt us as much as it would an African American, and initially I was more offended at being called lazy, but the tone in the man's voice as he said that last word, and his vitriol, stayed with me.

We didn't have a confrontation with that man, but I began to think about that word. The intent of that word gave it power. Shortly after that trip to the beach, another man, an Asian man, started to throw that epithet at me when he saw me walking around Blacktown. This man used to chase me with it, splashing the poison of that word on my back as I walked around.

I realised then that, no matter how much work I did to become an Australian, there would be some people who would never accept me. Even if I assimilated in every way, the darkness of my skin would preclude me from being considered Australian by a select group of Australians.

In my lighter moments, I recognised that it was only a small – but uncomfortably loud – section of Australians who thought that way. I knew that for every crazy old

Bondi man there were a dozen Geoff Hichersons. But, in my heavier moments, I started to wonder why I was working so hard on my studies, if I would always be defined by the darkness of my skin.

In 2001, I finished my TAFE course and received a qualification that was the equivalent of a high school certificate. I could now start to think about further education, and possibly even a vocation. I'd only ever thought about doing three things with my life – fighting, fishing and raising cattle, but I knew I didn't want a career in Australia doing any of those things. The problem was, I didn't have any idea of what else I could do, except a secret vocational dream that seemed so preposterous that I'd not spoken to anyone about it.

Then, one day, an Italian friend from my football club told me that his son was about to enrol in a one-year accounting course, and that I would do well to do the same. I told him I thought it was unlikely that I'd be able to keep up with a course like that but this friend promised that he and his son would help make sure that I passed.

I had never even thought about accounting as a concept, let alone a career. I had almost no experience with mathematics. Apart from a little foundational stuff we did at TAFE, the extent of my math studies had been memorising the multiplication tables that were printed on the workbooks that we were sometimes given when we studied English in Kakuma. Accounting, in principle, seemed to tick all of the boxes I wanted to tick in a career though. I wanted a job that was in an office – a regular job that would bring a regular wage. I was striving to get to middle Australia, and there didn't seem to be anywhere closer to the middle than accounting.

John had stressed that I should consider further study when I finished my TAFE course. When I told John about this accounting course, and the friend at football who said he would help me, John unequivocally told me I should do the course.

'It's with help that people like us will get ahead,' John told me. 'If help is there from someone you trust, you grab it with both hands.' It was a very Sudanese way of looking at things, as it's through clan or tribal connections that almost everything gets done back in Sudan.

I told John that I thought I didn't have the language skills or scholarly instinct to do accounting, but John didn't believe me on either count:

'The good thing about numbers is that they are the same in every language, and as far as you being a scholar – you won't have spent as much time in the classroom as the rest of the students, but I'd be surprised if they'd learned as much in their lives as you have. Also, your English is improving quickly, much faster than mine is. You always had an incredible brain for languages.'

John and I spoke as much English to each other as possible, but if something really needed to be said, we would speak in our mother language. So this conversation, like all our serious conversations, was spoken in the Dinka language.

John told me that he thought I would be a better student than him. I didn't believe that. John was a hustler, in the best sense of the word. He was relentless when he set his mind to something. He was not one to 'blow smoke up my arse' though, to use a recently acquired Australianism, and he wasn't going to have me commit to something he didn't think I could achieve.

I enrolled in an Advanced Diploma in Accounting the next day. It was an epochal time for both John and me. While I was starting my academic life, John was trying to begin his professional life, but even though he had climbed the academic rungs of his ladder, the professional footholds above him proved elusive.

Despite being a man of incredible drive and intelligence who spoke six languages, John could find no work except in a factory in Penrith. With each shift in that job, John's incredible moxie started to erode, ground down by life's unfairness – an unfairness he thought he'd escaped by coming to Australia.

John never stopped trying, though – attending meetings, sending resumes and petitioning aid organisations. The offers eventually came in, but only for work in East Africa, where John feared to return.

For my part, I threw myself into my accounting course and I found it close to being insurmountably difficult. True to his word, though, my Italian friend and his son never let me get too far behind, taking me back to their place many nights after school and filling me with coffee and study until I had caught up. Even though I completed the course with moderate grades, I always suspected I would be a bad accountant. My suspicions were confirmed after Geoff helped me get a job in the accounting department of the Marist Brothers' charity that had helped bring me to Australia.

I tried hard in that job, because I appreciated the opportunity to help an organisation that had done so much for me, but there were never going to be any songs about my incredible book-balancing. It just wasn't in my blood. I enjoyed having a full-time job, and the pay that accompanied it, though.

The rest of my African friends had started day jobs by then also, and we began going out regularly at night in the city and Kings Cross. None of us boys who used to meet at Lamin's place were drinkers, but we enjoyed going to bars and clubs, meeting girls and dancing, like most other young Australian men.

The word nigger was apparently even easier to unleash at night, and when we walked through the neon-lit Sydney streets, we'd hear it almost every night.

Sometimes there were fights, often with groups of Middle Eastern men. I would have imagined there would have been a fraternal bond between us, as some of them most likely came to Australia because they or their parents were also escaping a war, but that wasn't the case. The fights didn't stop us from going out, though. We weren't going to be chased away like that.

There was conflict at home, too. The relationship between Elizabeth and John was going from fractious to broken, in no small part because John was ill equipped to raise his children. The axiom about it taking a village to raise a child was literally true in Dinka culture, but the men in the village only took a role when the children were older than Josh and Guet were at that stage.

Soon the arguing between John and Elizabeth became intolerable for me. I sat down with John one evening and told him that I couldn't stand it anymore.

'You brought me to this country and you asked me to become soft, so I could fit in. I was a soldier, and you asked me to become a peaceful family man. I did that,' I told John. 'Now you're smashing that peace and family into pieces.'

John didn't disagree with me – he knew his transition into Australian society hadn't been an easy one – but, as the older brother, he couldn't take a backward step either. He was prideful and he told me that if I wanted to leave his house, I was welcome to do so.

At that stage, another family member had joined us, my uncle Philip Nyuon Akau, who had come to Australia as a refugee and was now studying for a bachelor's degree in engineering, which would eventually lead to a master's concentrating on irrigation.

'Mac cares about you, and he's worried about you,' Philip told me when John and I had separated. All of our Sudanese family referred to John as 'Mac', his Sudanese name.

'I worry about you too. You go out too much, you spend too much time with your friends, you don't seem happy. Neither you nor Mac seem happy, and that to me seems . . . unnecessary.'

Philip had always been a wise one. Even when I was back in my village, I'd look at him as an exemplar, no matter what the subject was. It was Philip who'd taught me how to bake the mud cows I loved to make in the sun so they could take form and solidity and not crumble in my hands.

I knew that John was unhappy, but I hadn't entertained the possibility that perhaps I wasn't happy either. I know in retrospect that I hadn't really been happy since I'd arrived in Australia, but I also knew that I had no problem being unhappy, as I'd not thought I should be happy. When we came to Australia John stressed to us, over and over, that getting to Australia was just a beginning. He used to tell me that when I got to Australia, there would only be work ahead of me, and he was right, but talking to Philip, I realised there could potentially be something else for me. Perhaps it was time for me to think about what I actually wanted for my life.

It seemed that for much of my life up until that point, I'd been subject to the volition of others – be they the SPLA, or John – but maybe now it was time to think about what I actually wanted from this new Australian start.

I thought and thought about it and I only came up with two answers. The first was that I no longer wanted to live with John and Elizabeth. I loved both of them, and I loved Josh and Guet too, but being in that house of perpetual discontent was poisoning me. I also decided that accounting would only ever be a job for me, not a career.

It seemed the two realisations were at odds with each other. If I were to get my own place, I'd need money, but if I wanted to have money, I'd need to keep my job. Or perhaps I could take another job? I did just that. I quit my accounting job, and took a position at the Red Lea chicken factory, taking chickens from their cages and putting them in trucks. All day, moving chooks from cage to truck.

I preferred that work to accounting, even if I stank of chicken shit all the time, regardless of how much I scrubbed, and how much deodorant I applied. I got my own place too, a tiny one-bedder in Blacktown, which was within cycling distance from the Red Lea facility.

Shortly after that, John left – the overseas contracts that he was being offered were too lucrative, and John desperately wanted to be able to make some money. The first position he took was in Somalia, but the second was in Sudan, working on a project just a few hundred kilometres west from where we were born.

In that period there had been a lull in the war, and both the SPLA and Sudanese government had gone back to the negotiating table. It was a time of rehabilitation and infrastructure building for Sudan – one of the first in some decades – but it was not exactly what you would call a time of peace.

I thought John's decision to go back to Sudan was extremely irresponsible. Elizabeth thought the same, and threatened to leave John, but he could not be moved on the subject. Even now I think John should have stayed in Australia, but I also have an adult's understanding of debt, opportunity and responsibility, and I feel more strongly the pressures John must have felt when he made his decision.

John's contract in Sudan was with Oxfam, working on a humanitarian project in the province of Bahr el Ghazal. There he had three resources in abundance that were greatly coveted: four-wheel drives, diesel fuels and Codan field radios. Of course, eventually an SPLA strongman came to John to relieve him of all three, and John tried to explain that he couldn't simply let the SPLA have the fuel, cars or radio, but that he and his team could bring much-needed food and agricultural supplies to the region.

The deal was not amenable to the SPLA. They came back with soldiers, seized the cars, fuel and radios and beat John unconscious. When he came to he was in a sheer-walled pit filled with human excrement in a military camp. There he wallowed and wasted for days, before being transferred to an SPLA jail. I think the only thing that kept him from being killed was his Australian citizenship.

It took some days for an Australian consular representative to be dispatched to save John. The Australian consulate in Nairobi initially tried to secure John's release remotely, but the SPLA would not even admit that he was in detention and, later, when there was no doubt where John was, they flatly refused the request, telling the consulate that John was South Sudanese, not Australian, and therefore subject to their total authority.

Eventually John was released, and soon was in an intensive care unit in Nairobi, on the verge of death. When he was well enough to return to Sydney he did so, and when I saw him, he looked like an old man. John had added to his old scars, with fractures of the head and facial lacerations, and was also suffering a malady that would change his whole life.

During his time in that pit of shit, the skin condition John had suffered during the war – most likely a rare autoimmune disease – became far more acute. John's skin now cracked and fissured when he was in even mild cold, and he could not bear to be in air conditioning, let alone an Australian winter.

John would now forever be tied to Africa, or that was at least the way John saw it. As broken and sick as he was when he came back, John was resolved to return to Sudan.

I thought it seemed a suicidal impulse to go back, even in this time of relative 'peace'. There were so many ways to die, even if John hadn't randomly fallen afoul of some of the more brutal elements of the SPLA, the people who would want to see John dead were gaining power in the SPLA. John had held some of the most sensitive information when he was a radio operator during the war. He had been a conduit between Dr John Garang and his deputy Salva Kiir during the brutal height of the war, and it wasn't unusual for those who knew where bodies were buried to wind up dead themselves. Sudan was in John's blood though, literally and figuratively.

Elizabeth was incandescently angry with John's decision. John told her that she had no right to be and that the wife's job was to care, and the man's job was to provide, wherever he could. I didn't stick around when they started tearing strips off each other again.

I started to understand John's desire to return to Sudan. While in Australia, I'd become privy to information about the ways that my family had been targeted by certain parts of the SPLA. Family members had been routinely found dead if they had the audacity to gain an education or some significant status around Bor and Jonglei, and those killings were still happening.

I thought it was an outrage, and seeing my brother broken and beaten, did something to me. It made me want to go back to Sudan with John and try to protect our family, which John was trying to do now physically and financially.

I'd not thought much about our family in Sudan before, but I started to think about them more around this time. I told John that one day I wanted to go back to Sudan and right all the wrongs that had been done to John and our family.

'What does that mean?' John asked me.

'Prosecute the people responsible if we can.'

'And if . . . and when we can't?'

I just shrugged my shoulders. It was only a few years since I had been in the army, and I thought that if those men were killed, then that would be a just outcome. John made me promise that I wouldn't return to Sudan. He told me that I was too outspoken, with too much of a black and white understanding of morality. He told me that my life wasn't in Sudan, like his had to be.

Before the cold of winter could set in, John took another contract in Sudan and left us. Elizabeth had told John that she was finished with him; she'd met another Sudanese man who she would eventually have two children with.

I think John's pride had been deeply bruised in Australia, but in Africa I suspected he could feel like a man again. And that was probably doubly true when he found that Elizabeth was with another man.

Eventually John would have another Australian love too – Elizabeth's cousin, whom he had a child with. When Elizabeth heard about this child, her pride was at least equally hurt and she forswore that John would only be in her life as the father of her children. Some couples, however, are bound in a reason-defying way, and that was true of John and Elizabeth. They had another child in 2008 – a girl they named Aluel.

John was in Sudan when the Sudanese peace agreement was finally signed. In the years before the agreement, the pointless, bloody taking and retaking of places like Torit and Kapoeta had stopped, and the south had settled into a state of restless stalemate. The SPLA had taken almost the entire south of Sudan, except some major population centres like Juba and Bor, which the northern-led government had to resupply from the air at great difficulty and expense.

The SPLA was also operating in the north, in potential breakaway areas like the Nuba Mountains and the Blue Nile. The fighting in those areas threatened to open up again a full-scale, multi-fronted war, and that was something the north wanted to avoid if at all possible.

After twenty-two years of constant war, in which an estimated two million people were killed, legal peace came to Sudan on 9 January 2005. The agreement stipulated that the north could not insist on sharia law in the south – the root cause of the war – and that Khartoum would allow for a referendum on the potential independence of the south. The SPLA was to stop attacking the oilfields that would now benefit both north and south, and also demobilise all of their remaining child soldiers. Many of those soldiers were sent home, but many reported to barracks again a few weeks later.

When I came to Australia, we were some of only a handful of Sudanese in Sydney, but by the time the peace agreement had been signed six years later, the refugee community had swollen. When the official reconciliation between north and south was announced, the Sudanese diaspora partied through the day and night across Western Sydney, from Sydney Olympic Park to Granville, and of course Blacktown, where the bulk of the Australian–Sudanese had resettled.

We danced, sang Sudanese songs and played football, and I shared food and drink with Nuer and Dinka alike – and even people from the north. I got home in the early hours of the morning and, as I lay in my bed, I wondered what a cessation in the fighting might mean for John and my mother. I also wondered if I would now be able to free myself from my nightmares. Of course, after a couple of hours of sleep, I was right back in Kapoeta, waiting for bullets, artillery and death to greet me.

Chapter Eight

SOME TO JUSTICE, SOME TO FATE

After the peace was signed into law, many of the Sudanese who had run to Australia planned their return. The peace agreement stipulated that the south would have limited autonomy for six years, paving the way for a referendum on independence that was planned for 2011.

In my lifetime there had never been a time of hope in the south of Sudan like that time. John came back to Sydney after the peace agreement but by then I realised he was not returning to us in a permanent way.

'There will be a new country, Deng, and that will be my home,' he said.

I had mixed feelings about what John was doing. I understood his excitement about the possibility of the birth of this new country, and that he now felt fealty to our family in Sudan, but John had laid roots in Australia. He had a family here – children – and that meant he had responsibility. I was there for John's children, but I was not their father. I couldn't completely condemn him, though. After all, he wasn't moving to the United States, but back to the villages of my youth to improve the war-ravaged lives of the people living there, and there were also many months that he couldn't live in Sydney anyway because of his skin condition.

Before he left I sought John out for advice. I had decided I wanted to apply for a course of university study and, as the graduate of an Australian university, I wanted to know which school John thought I should apply for. John told me that the answer would depend on what field of study I was looking to take on.

I told John I wanted to study environmental science. It was a dream I'd harboured for years without ever admitting. The Nile River has been the wet centre of my soul since I was born, and I thought about it often. During the war I'd heard of a plan the north had to divert water through the Sudd wetlands – a tributary of the Nile – back up to the north of Sudan and Egypt. The project, which was to be called the Jonglei Canal, would essentially end fishing and agriculture as many of us Dinka knew it.

As I got older I started to understand that that project would have been a cultural genocide for our people. The canal project was only abandoned when the war consumed the south, and I'm sure would have been resumed if the north had managed to destroy the SPLA.

A giant abandoned French-made digger sitting out in the Jonglei swamps is all that remains of the project, but I often thought about what Sudan would have been like for a Dinka fisherman's son in a land with no access to fish or grazing ground for our cows.

The canal was an omnipresent thought in my mind, even though I'd expunged most other thoughts of Africa. When I told John of my prospective field of study he told me, in no uncertain terms, that it was something I should not dedicate years to.

'The intention is right, but the execution isn't. Deng, people who make decisions about projects like the Jonglei Canal aren't environmental scientists,' John said. 'They're politicians or lawyers. I'd always seen you as a lawyer.'

'A lawyer? I couldn't handle being an accountant, and you think I could be a lawyer?'

'I do. I've never met anyone as argumentative as you,' he said with a chuckle. 'Listen. You left the village when you were just a little boy, but you know all the ins and outs of Dinka-Bor law better than anyone.'

'That's just knowing the songs,' I said.

'Songs, books . . . what's the difference? What were your best courses when you studied accounting?'

It was true that the courses I found easiest were those looking at taxation law.

'And when an environmental impact study is done on a project like the Jonglei Canal, who do you think uses that study to get a state like Sudan to act against their self-interest? Of course it is the lawyers, and only the lawyers.'

I'd never entertained the possibility of studying law but, while I'd lost respect for John in some ways, I'd gained respect for him in others. I knew he knew me better than anyone else in the world. Still, I didn't think I could study law, and when I told my friends they agreed with me, laughing at the possibility.

They thought perhaps I would be able to do law in five or ten years' time – when my English had improved considerably. John said that my friends were just buying into a theme that some people in a position of privilege like to perpetuate so people like me – people like us African kids, us kids from Western Sydney – don't come into their hallowed halls, and take their desirable jobs.

'You're a hard worker, Deng. When you set your mind to doing something, you can do it, including this.'

That was perhaps the last advice I ever took from John, but it was the best, and the most fruitful. I applied to study law at three universities: the University of New England, Western Sydney University and Macquarie University. My hopes were hanging on Macquarie as of the three it had the most prestigious law school.

My preferences were confused, however, when one of Macquarie's law professors, Drew Fraser, wrote a letter to a newspaper suggesting that it would be a disaster admitting more Sudanese refugees into Australia because, 'experience practically everywhere in the world shows us that an expanding black population is a sure-fire recipe for increases in crime, violence and other social problems'.

Fraser's comments incited some media interest, and he used the platform not to back away from his statement, but to charge onward, claiming that there was research that proves that black people have significantly lower IQs than white people, especially sub-Saharan African people like me.

Professor Fraser's comment hurt me more than being called a nigger. This was a learned man, with sway in the community, not some bitter old man, or a drunk kid on a bender.

When Macquarie's acting vice-chancellor refused to condemn Fraser's views – instead citing academic freedoms as a defence for Fraser's comments, which would be undiscernible mixed in with lines from *Mein Kampf* – I resolved not to take up an offer of admission, should I get one from Macquarie, regardless of how it might look on a future CV.

I ended up receiving offers from all three universities, and immediately threw the offer from Macquarie in the bin.

Such was my excitement at being offered a spot to study law at Western Sydney University that I barely even thought about the Macquarie offer, until I told John about my multiple offers.

'You will take up the Macquarie offer then, yes?' he asked.

'Absolutely not.' He knew why, too. I doubt there were any Sudanese who'd not heard about the comments and the university's response.

'You will take that offer,' John said, with anger in his voice, as though I was taking something away from him. He composed himself.

'In a few years' time, this racism stuff will all be forgotten, and you will have a better degree than the one you would get at Western Sydney University.'

'I won't have forgotten.'

'Sometimes you have to compromise, Deng. That's the secret to life.'

I wasn't going to budge. If I were to be a lawyer, I planned to be a lawyer who was principled, not one who worked in margins of moral compromise. I couldn't start this new career by ignoring my disgust for racism and tribalism.

The Macquarie conundrum made me realise that I'd learned a lot since I'd arrived in Australia. When I was a child in Sudan, I assumed that the *kawaja* and the Arabs were all completely different species from my family and me. I even thought the Shilluk and the Nuer, and the Toposa were a different species from me. If I'd known anything about DNA, I would have assumed that theirs curled differently, causing them to behave in a different fashion from me, eat differently, drink differently, hurt differently and love differently. It was that assumed difference that allowed me to be trained to kill them.

I think the idea that people are inherently anything – good, bad, violent, stupid, blessed or expendable – is the most dangerous idea in the world. I would not spend years on the campus of a university that didn't understand that.

I also argued with John that accommodating racist ideas was to be intellectually bankrupt, so perhaps the Western Sydney University degree would be more worthwhile than a Macquarie University degree when I graduated.

John was slowly but surely convinced, or at least he was convinced that I was not likely to budge. As I saw him relent, I thought to myself – perhaps I did have what it would take to become a lawyer.

I accepted the offer from Western Sydney University, but that offer came with the caveat that it would be rescinded if I failed any of my core first-year units. I doubled up my English studies, and engaged a private tutor, in preparation for my first day at WSU.

I stepped onto the campus still not knowing if I could complete my course. I would try, though. I'd had another dramatic upswing in my English comprehension, but I still found some of the terms used in my first-year textbooks confounding, and law is almost all about careful reading.

My boys initially thought my legal aspirations were a joke, but they supported me once the course began. I still saw the boys, but it was usually over the top of a textbook. I took my reading everywhere – on the bus and train, to dinners at Lamin's place, even to football practice, so I could read while I stretched. I took endless notes, also, writing down any words or terms that I didn't understand, making sure that I looked them up later and was able to use them correctly in future instances.

I enjoyed law a lot. During my first year of study, it

occurred to me that I had actually started life in a highly structured environment and was now returning to one.

While the Dinka do not have a written legal canon, there were very rigid and adhered-to laws regarding everything from murder and theft to property disputes and defamation. Even when looked at from afar, Dinka law is a beautiful thing, composed for the benefit of the land, the river, the cattle and the people. Then there was the war. There was only one law in the war, and that law was that the war is bigger than you. The war served almost no people, scorched the earth, scattered and killed the cattle, and poisoned the river.

I was drunk on the law of the war when I came to Australia, but I sobered up as I learned more of the rules and language of the country that had welcomed me. As I started to learn the Australian laws, I found that they were like Dinka law, but instead of being in the service of people and land, it was in the service of people and of precedent.

In that first year of law the reading was extensive, the language often confusing and arcane, and there were few nights where my eyes didn't ache at the end of all the reading, but Australian law made sense to me – from intent to application. I passed all my core classes in the first year of my studies, allowing me to continue with my degree, but I did fail a 'law foundation' class. The failure stemmed from my refusal to back away from an ethical stance I took in class.

A brilliant academic named Dr Michael Head, who was well known in Australian socialist circles, and contributed readily and intelligently to socialist journals, conducted the class and posed this theoretical problem to us:

'A bomb has been placed in a passenger jet with 200 people on board. It's primed to explode shortly. A suspect has been found, but he's not cooperating with the police. How far outside of the bounds of Australian law can you morally operate with this suspect?'

The opinion of the room was the opinion that was obviously sought by Dr Head: there is no wiggle room. The law is the law. I had another, dissenting view.

'I would torture him,' I told Dr Head.

'How can you be sure you have the right man? And even then, how would you know that the information was right?' my tutor asked.

'I know that people lie when under extreme duress. I have tortured and I have been tortured, but it would be worth the chance that you may get some information that could save the people on that flight.'

'That answer is categorically wrong, Deng, I'm sorry.'

Dr Head explained his reasoning. The law has to be allowed to be imperfect in singular situations. It moves, and bends over time, but it does not break.

'Do you understand?' Dr Head asked.

'I do, but I would still torture this man. And I would also torture his family, if it was needed.'

I was starting to believe in human rights, but I believed in a utilitarian version of human rights. I believed in the golden mean – the greatest good for the greatest number. I would not be budged.

The argument continued throughout the course. Both Dr Head and I thought we were arguing to the benefit of the greatest good for the greatest number, and I made impassioned but brutal arguments. I was only a handful of years removed from my time in the military, and not just a military, but one of the most ruthless militaries in the world. Arguments of bombs and death were not abstract for me.

While we were debating theoretical aviation death in Australia, the real thing was happening in South Sudan.

In my first year of university, Dr John Garang, who was the head of state in waiting, died along with six colleagues and seven crew members when his helicopter crashed flying between Uganda and Sudan in the middle of 2005.

Officially Garang died due to pilot error and poor weather, but many believe he was murdered, including his wife Rebecca Garang, who said while giving a speech in 2007: 'When my husband died, I did not come out openly and say he was killed because I knew the consequences. At the back of my mind, I knew my husband had been assassinated.'

If Garang was killed, then who killed him? The list of possible assassins is a long one, from the Sudanese government, which Garang was the vice-president of; to Joseph Kony's Lord's Resistance Army, which had a heavy presence in the area where the helicopter went down; to myriad SPLA actors, be they Nuer or Dinka.

Garang was both beloved and contentious. He was a gregarious, intelligent leader, and he was also my ideological north star for the first half of my life, but he was also a man whose face I saw when I had nightmares in which men were executed in front of me. Garang's family tortured mine, too, and that was something I thought about every time I saw John's scars, or when he struggled to get out of a chair.

I had very mixed feelings about Dr Garang, and those feelings bubbled and boiled when I heard about his death. Still, there was too much of the SPLA in me to say that

I wouldn't have approved the torture of whomever it was that killed him, if he was, indeed, murdered.

I failed that ethics course. I recognise now that my arguments must have been jarring in peaceful Australia, but I would also argue that the course was always going to be a little harder for me than the other people in that class. A German military strategist once said that – 'no battle plan survives contact with the enemy', and I would say that's true of a completely conventional understanding of ethics and morality.

I passed the rest of my first-year courses, however, and I was off to my second year of studies. Then things became even more difficult, as the course work became more voluminous and complex. I fell behind, and started filing assignments late. I may have dropped out except that the dean and deputy dean of the law school – Professor Michael Adams and Dr Stephen Janes – took a personal interest in me, and helped me immensely.

They recognised that I was working hard, but that the cards were stacked against me somewhat, with my English still a work in progress and the academic rigour of a law degree a relatively new concept to me. They gave me no special treatment, but they monitored my progress, giving me a gentle push when it looked like I was going to fall too far behind. With those great men taking a personal interest in me, I thought it would have been a great dishonour to fail in my studies, so I redoubled my efforts.

I knew that the semesters were only going to become increasingly difficult and that things would have to change if I was to graduate. I decided I was going to return to the attitude I had as a boy soldier. When I was in the SPLA I would set a detailed plan for what I was going to do that day as soon as I woke. That was the only way to survive. I started doing the same thing at university.

In the army there was never any food during the day, so I decided to stop eating at the campus. We slept very little when we were in the army too, so I started to go to bed very late and woke very early. That last measure actually helped me become more rested because when I was extremely fatigued I found I had far fewer nightmares.

The only activity I routinely kept up while at WSU was football, which was also something I'd done in the army. I played football and studied and attended lectures, and had time with Elizabeth and the kids, and that was the whole sum of my life.

Then, one day, I finished my degree. As the graduation came closer and closer, I actually believed less and less that I would be handed a degree. I never thought gaining a law degree could be possible, even as I was picking up my gown and mortarboard. John had thought it possible, but

I never really believed him. I had still seen myself as the grubby-faced child I'd been, with an AK-47 in his hands and death in his core, even as I progressed through year after year of law.

I spoke to John every week while studying, and at times of particular stress, I would call him every day. He was a calming presence on the phone. He hadn't been when I was living with him, but things were different after he moved permanently back to South Sudan. I could never respect his decision to permanently move away from his children, but he was certainly more at peace in Africa, and more himself.

John flew back to Australia for my graduation and was incandescently happy when I was handed my degree. There were so many gates to that moment that I wouldn't have been able to get through without John's help. None of it would have been possible without him. I told him that night that, even though he had mostly been in Africa while I was studying, I wouldn't have been able to get the degree without him.

He was so proud.

There were all kinds of friends and family at the graduation. After the ceremony we went to a church in Blacktown for a party of Dinka music and Sudanese food. People gave speeches too, and there was even one from James Mading Mabil, my sometimes harsh, sometimes angelic squad leader from the war. He now lived in Sydney too, and I was very happy that I could share my triumphant moment with him.

Seeing so many people from my youth, I started to think about home. I was keen to start my career, but I was also, for the first time, yearning to go back to my village. I'd been asking John a lot of questions about home before my graduation, and I told him I was thinking about returning to South Sudan. Once again, he told me, in no uncertain terms, not to return.

'Your sun is rising now, Deng, and you must start work. We are technically a country in peace, but there is still danger. When you are established, and the guns have been put away, that will be the time.'

'Then I would be grey and old, if such a time comes at all,' I laughed.

The South Sudanese would usually not dare to talk about a time when the guns had been stowed. There had always been a violent struggle for power within the SPLA, which had only been amplified with a whole nation's worth of resources and power up for grabs while the framework of independence and statehood was being established.

By the time of my graduation, most South Sudanese people believed that two contentious, powerful leaders – Riek Machar and Salva Kiir – would lead the country into another civil war, with the dividing line being roughly drawn between the Dinka tribe and the Nuer tribe.

Machar, the commander of the SPLA breakaway group that had killed so many in Bor during the war, had become the vice-president of South Sudan, and when he had ordered that the supposedly magical *dang* (a rod belonging to the Nuer prophet Ngundeng Bong) be returned from London to Juba, and started holding it aloft like Moses, we knew he was not going to be happy with his station as vice-president.

The *dang* was a powerful magical item in the eyes of the Nuer. Made of tamarind wood and copper, the three-foot rod had been the prize possession of Ngundeng Bong and its potency was intertwined with the prophet's most famous proclamation – that a left-handed Nuer would best a bearded man in a war that would allow a new nation to rise. Machar was left-handed, the new president, Salva Kiir, was bearded – unusual for a South Sudanese man. The symbolism of the return of the *dang* was obvious.

I knew the danger, but I still wanted to visit. I had started to think more and more about my mother. For a long time I'd managed to expunge thoughts of Athieu Akau Deng, safe in the knowledge that she had a large family to look after, but now I started to entertain the possibility of a return. I wanted to see John as well. John was only prone to self-promotion when it was needed, and so I had heard only a small part of his African story, which I understood was one of success. I knew that John had co-founded an NGO that aimed to help eradicate disease from southern Sudanese cattle herds, but he also had a number of other businesses including a hotel, a small airline and a four-wheel drive importation business.

John was far from the only person from my tribe who had returned from Australia educated and activated, pouring their new skills into the maw of a new nation forged by war. Perhaps I could help too, and also be reunited with my mother and brother.

As we spoke further, John became more adamant that I should not return; in fact, he strictly forbade it. He said that I had momentum now in Australia, and that I must continue with work or further studies. He said it over and over and I knew he was right, but once the possibility of a return became an idea in my mind, it only grew.

After graduating I picked up a job as a lawyer at a firm called Grace Legal and instantly I liked the day-to-day work. Each case was both technical and human, and in each instance, resolution changed lives. I was often helping people – first generation Australians – in legal cases, and it was rewarding work. I hadn't been a natural student, but practising law was something I truly loved. I couldn't, however, stop thinking about South Sudan, and my mum and John and how I might be able to help there.

•

In 2011 I arranged to take leave, and I bought a ticket to Juba. My flight went through Dubai, and it was only at that airport that I told John – or anyone in South Sudan – that I was coming. He was at the airport to pick me up, and gently berated me, before giving me a warm welcome.

'Welcome home, Little Swallow.'

Although he never said it, I think John appreciated being able to show me what he'd managed to build. In Australia, John had always been behind the financial eight ball, despite being a naturally industrious and hard-working man. Often, while he was studying, John had had to resort to Centrelink payments to feed his children, and getting handouts made him ornery and disoriented. It was so far from what he had planned while he dreamed in Kakuma.

In South Sudan he was the owner or co-owner of a number of thriving businesses, including a brickmaking business that could barely keep up in the reconstructive environment that was post-war Juba. I had had my problems with John, combining the resentment a teenager can have for both a father and a brother, but I had always loved him, and I was buoyed to see him the successful man he was always destined to be, but somehow couldn't be in Australia.

I worked with John for a little while – helping put together a tally of his assets and mediating in a minor industrial matter between his brickmaking business and its workers. I'll never forget that time. John wore success very well – it matched his personality. For a little while I even stopped getting on his case about his children, which was always the main point of disagreement between us.

Part of me also enjoyed seeing the independent South Sudanese flag flying high across the capital, and seeing Jeep-bound SPLA soldiers criss-crossing the city with impunity. Only part of me, mind you. I still couldn't fully get behind the idea that what had been done to win the war was completely justified, and the air of militarised paranoia that lingered in Juba was disconcerting for someone who'd spent so much time in Australia.

After a little time in Juba, I left John – who was then working seven days a week – and flew to Bor, and onward to my village and my mother. Both time and the war had aged my mother, but she was undeniably the incredible woman who had reluctantly sent me off to war with a package of food more than twenty years earlier. She greeted me with a hug and we wept. There was still such a familiarity in her touch and voice and smile. It was in my DNA.

We had so much to catch up on. I wanted to know about her life, but she said that little else but war had happened to her and she didn't want to talk about that. I told her about my life in Australia, and my work and studies and the law.

I stayed in the village for a couple of weeks and quickly realised how attached I'd become to the ease of western life. I struggled without electricity, or running water and an actual bed. I wondered if I could ever live the village life again, and if I could ever marry traditionally. I'd always assumed I could, but with each day in the dust, I started to wonder. The real shock in that first trip though, was how few people from my childhood remained in the village. So many had been killed in the war and the massacres, and so many more had been scattered within or outside Sudan's borders.

I asked my mother about what had happened to her when the Nuer attacked Bor in 1991 – the main incident that led to the villages feeling so empty. She said she didn't want to talk about it, but near the end of my trip she said that I should probably know some details and how she got away.

A niece of mine named Bouth Anyagat had led my mother across the Nile to the swampy east bank during the fighting. *Bouth* means 'leftovers' in Dinka, and *Anyagat* means 'traitor' – she had been named so because at that stage almost every other child had been sent away to fight in the war, or had run away, or had been killed.

Across the river a tribe of marsh dwellers and fishermen called the Dinka-Aliab sheltered my mother. The Nuer were skilled warriors, but they were not adept at marine combat, and my mother stayed safe with the Dinka-Aliab until she received word she could return to our bank. There she found the village and the whole region littered with the dead. Most of the dead had been killed by machetes or spears. All had been left to rot where they had been massacred. The few men and boys who were not off in the war had been left to try to defend the villages, so it was the women and girls, like my mother and Bouth Anyagat, who were left to dig and fill the graves.

While I was staying in the village, I was shocked at how alone my mother was. My youngest brother Akau had just joined the army and, although she'd birthed a considerable brood, she now only had grandchildren to look after her. I asked her if she would ever consider coming to Australia, but she said moving would be impossible for her.

'I'm an old woman now,' she said. 'And I have lived my entire life here. I'll die here also. I am at that stage in life.'

On my way back to Australia, I stopped off in Juba and spoke to John about my mum. I told John that I was considering getting a job in Bor, so that I could look after her.

'Village life isn't easy, but it's the life she's chosen, Deng,' John told me. 'I think you should do what she wants you to do. She wants you to go back to Australia and make something of yourself.'

I knew that was what she wanted. While I was with her, Mum had often complained that she was still alive, while so many of the younger generation were dead. She said it was unnatural. I calmed her by telling her that nothing was going to happen to me in Australia.

I had been sending money home for years, but I wondered if that was enough. I spoke to John about the possibility of Mum moving to Australia. He just laughed.

'Did you talk to her about it?' he asked.

I nodded.

'And what did she say? Deng, you need to respect her wishes.'

He was right. John was a young man when he came to Australia, and the difference in the way of life was almost too shocking even for him. My mother had lived her whole life in a tiny, remote African village. She refused to relocate to Juba, just 200 kilometres south, so she was not going to live in Australia, which was culturally and geographically a world away.

I realised I couldn't compare her life to mine, and that I shouldn't apply my understanding of quality of life to hers.

Part of the reason I was so concerned about my mother was the feeling of unease in the South Sudanese capital. There were more guns in Juba, and more nervous looks. There were mutters about blood feuds everywhere, and tribal discontent.

It felt to me as though the capital was like an upset stomach, ready to let loose something vile.

I returned to Sydney but resolved I would go back to see my mother again, and soon. While I worked, I looked into master's courses that I might do, but I thought more and more about John and my mother and the new nation that was precariously positioned between the hill of reconstruction and the precipice of war.

My thoughts about South Sudan also made me think more about the plight of African refugees. Even though I had been a refugee myself, both John and I were dedicated solely to the progression of our own lives, and were not particularly involved in the plight of other refugees. Now I was in a position to help, so I started to feel as though I should. I took on as much pro bono work as I could, finding it especially difficult to turn down work representing South Sudanese men and women. Later that year I was delighted and shocked to learn that I'd been nominated for the New South Wales Law Society Justice Medal.

I returned to South Sudan again in 2012, once again against John's wishes. Once again when I arrived in Juba, John admonished me briefly and then greeted me warmly.

Before I'd left Australia I had been thinking a lot about whether a man as African as me could ever be accepted in Australia, and more specifically in the legal profession. Yes, there were many kind people who had not only accepted me but helped me in my career, but there were also some – and at the highest level too – who saw me as somewhat inferior because of my skin and accent. Before I had left for South Sudan I'd been pulled over in my car for no other reason than I was black, having to prove to a policeman that I owned the vehicle I was driving, and I'd also been sanctioned for purportedly offending a magistrate when I knew my behaviour was completely in line with normal, transactional court conversation.

It was strange but at the point where I was starting to get all that I'd worked for, I was beginning to wonder whether I actually belonged in the country that I lived in, or in the country that I'd fought for. Even just a couple of years after independence it was obvious that South Sudan was not going to be the shining example of Christian African excellence that George W. Bush and the American right

– great champions of South Sudanese independence – hoped it would be. But even though it was dangerous and likely to become more dangerous, in many ways it felt like home, especially during that second trip.

On that trip, I was far more comfortable with village life. I fished every day on the Nile while I was up in the villages, and spent lots of time at the cattle camps. I was honoured when a bull was slaughtered so we could feast and celebrate my return. I was seduced by South Sudan – by the music I heard as I went past villages, the ease of speaking my native languages, and the smell of the river. Yes, you could feel danger in South Sudan, but you could also feel hope.

I spent some time in Bor, which was the capital of Jonglei state, and where a number of my family members had taken up government positions. That's where I thought I might be best used, if I were to pick up a job in South Sudan.

As a new nation that was as much argued into existence by the UN and US as it was fought for by the SPLA, aid money gushed into South Sudan after independence. Travelling around the nation, however, there was very little evidence of any of the money leaving the capital. In Juba I had seen fleets of white Land Rovers zipping around, deploying *kawaja* here and there, but in Bor there wasn't even one paved road. In fact, there were no paved roads anywhere in South Sudan except the capital.

I wanted to deliver a gift to the governor of Jonglei – Kuol Manyang Juuk, a towering figure in the war. He was the commander of the SPLA forces in Torit, but before that he had held overall command of the areas around Bor in the 1980s. In fact, the ribbon of boys that took me away from my home was designed by Kuol Manyang.

I was related to Kuol Manyang but, despite that fact, he had most likely ordered the death of more of my family members than anyone else. He was known for being ruthless in battle, and just as ruthless when maintaining discipline in peacetime. Throughout the country, he was regarded as a viciously effective general and – for those so bold – he was also known as being passionately bloodthirsty.

Executions were common under Kuol Manyang's command, and family or tribal connections would rarely help you escape a firing squad bullet if you crossed him. He was a brutal man for a brutal season. I hoped that the season was changing, and that the man could change too.

I had bought a gorgeous, limited edition Cartier pen before leaving Sydney, and wanted to give it to Kuol Manyang in person and tell him that I hoped in the future he would have more call to use it than his gun.

A visit was arranged through family intermediaries, and I travelled to the governor's compound with my uncle, Philip Nyuon Akau, who had completed his engineering master's in Australia, and was back in South Sudan. He was hoping to help with some reconstruction projects near our village, and while we were waiting to meet with Kuol Manyang, we sat with a group of men who included Mayen Ngor, the state minister for agriculture – a man who I remembered from Pinyudo where he had also been in charge of agri-culture for a while.

I remembered him being a man of hustle and machi-nation, but little skill and knowledge. I'm sure that part of the reason there was so little food in the camp at Pinyudo was due to his incompetence. I vividly remember him ordering seeds be planted on ground that even I, an uneducated child, knew was barren.

He and Philip eventually started a conversation about irrigation, and soon Mayen was out of his depth. The minister resorted to an oft-heard defence in South Sudan:

'That's the problem with this country – foreigners coming to this country with western educations with little understanding of how our country really works.'

The men within earshot – who were sitting around idly, playing dominoes – agreed emphatically. The suggestion that men like my uncle and me – who had both fought for the SPLA – were foreigners stung bitterly. I also couldn't believe that these men couldn't recognise that an influx of foreign-found skills would be useful to the nation. I said nothing at the time, but I have thought of that offhand comment often since.

When I met with Kuol Manyang, he was happy to receive as fine a pen as the one I gave him, but he said he thought it was not yet time for him to replace his weapon. He said his gun was a part of him, and that, as a former soldier, I should know that as well as anyone.

Before my visit to the governor's office I had been seriously considering moving back to South Sudan, but the visit gave me an understanding of the difficulties that I would meet daily. When I told John about the meeting, he just laughed.

'I tried to tell you, Deng, you've become too used to the fairness and equality of Australia and Australians. I am proud that you have, but it would make it hard for you to live here.'

He was right. When a situation deviated from that fairness, then it would put me out of kilter until I had managed to rectify it, and unfairness would be something I would be dealing with daily in South Sudan, and would just have to accept.

When I returned home to Sydney I threw myself into my work. I decided to take on both the University of New South Wales and the University of Wollongong master's that I was offered, as well as taking on a substantial caseload at my new firm, LN Legal. I also kept up with my pro bono work twice a week. And then, about halfway through 2013, I became even busier after meeting a man named Joe Correy while defending a South Sudanese man in an aggravated assault case.

The South Sudanese man came to me after he had been arrested when a fight had broken out during a football game. Weapons had been used in the fight, specifically a crowbar and screwdrivers, and my client was one of nine African men who were charged, uniformly, by police after the incident.

The group had been charged en masse with rioting. The men were all looking at a short custodial sentence and a criminal record. Most of the charged men chose to take on the suggested pleas of guilty as offered by the police prosecution, and wear the sanction that would come. My client, however, thought he was not as culpable as some of the other men in the group.

The more I looked into the case, the more it seemed to me that the police had picked the not-uncommon narrative of 'a bunch of crazy black men went crazy', instead of taking the time to look at the individual actions and responsibilities of the nine different human beings involved in the incident.

Too often, those outside Africa group Africans collectively, without considering the individuals in a group. On a macro level, when considering something like a war or pandemic, it's important to keep in mind that every person who died did so after a unique and monumental losing battle, resulting in inimitable grief. It's also important to keep in mind that, on a micro level – say after a football brawl – each person involved had their own motivation, fears and culpability.

After doing my research into the football fight I found that there was an instigator, an aggressor and an escalator, and that, probably, my client was none of those things. At court, I approached the police prosecutor and indicated as such. I requested that my client be subject only to the affray charge with amended facts and after much convincing he eventually agreed. Then we moved to my favourite part of proceedings – the striking off of unfounded charges.

In the last few years I have picked up something of a weakness for expensive pens, but my favourite writing implement is the thick black texta I keep in my inside pocket when going to court. I pulled it out and started to whittle down the charges that had been levelled at my client but had not been proven. Line after line of culpability disappeared under my ink, and with it money and time that my client would have owed the state. It was, and still is, an indescribably wonderful feeling. When I was finished, a few sporadic lines of the original charge sheet remained.

It was then that I noticed the lawyer of the only other co-accused who had not taken the original Crown offer. This lawyer's name was Joe Correy, a kind-looking and energetic young lawyer of Lebanese descent, who had been retained by one of the other defendants. Joe had done almost exactly the same redacting job that I had. I held up my charge sheet and we shared a smile and a moment of mutual satisfaction.

Having negotiated the charges, it was now time to present our evidence to the court. Joe argued to the court that just because all of the men in the brawl had a similar skin tone that didn't mean they were all similarly culpable. Joe claimed that while his client had helped instigate the initial fracas – which almost anyone who'd played sport would probably be familiar with – the violence that necessitated these legal proceedings was a shock to his client, and that his client had indeed been a victim of it.

Correy had taken the time to break down, from moment to moment, what happened on the day of the brawl and argued that his client should not be sentenced to imprisonment. I could tell that Joe was looking for a similar outcome to the one I was looking for. I wasn't trying to have my client completely exonerated – I thought there was no getting away from the affray charges – but I didn't think he deserved to go to jail either.

Before I started law school I held a Pollyanna-ish assumption that everyone in Australia gets the legal defence they deserve. After a few years of working in the profession, I knew that that assumption was unfounded. I could see no holes in Joe's defence of his client though, just rigorous and complete reason. I was impressed. My submissions were eerily similar.

My client ended up receiving only a section-ten (dismissal) bond, which meant that although they were found guilty they wouldn't have a criminal record. Joe's client received a Community Service Order, an outstanding result. It was undoubtedly a winning outcome for both of us. Ironically, our clients were on opposing sides of the affray.

That evening Joe and I met over a few beers. Eventually the conversation moved to the paths that we saw ourselves taking in the law business. I saw myself becoming a barrister. It was something that my boss, Lyndon Nguyen, wished for me, and had said he would help me achieve. Joe said he saw himself setting up his own practice.

'I've just been waiting to find the right partner,' he said, clinking my glass.

I met the cheers and took a sip of my beer.

'So? What do you think?' he asked.

'Of what?' I was a little slow on the uptake. Joe laughed.

'Well . . . would you consider . . . looking into the possibility of becoming partners?'

Setting up a practice wasn't something I'd ever thought about until Joe asked. As soon as he did though, I instinctively knew it was the right thing to do. I agreed there and then to consider looking into the possibility. A few months later AC (or Adut–Correy) Law Group hung out its first shingle in Blacktown.

When I made the decision to set up shop with Joe, I thought my boss at the time, Lyndon Nguyen, would be happy for me. We'd worked from a place of mutual respect, Lyndon and me. He'd taken me on as something of a protégé, and had often said that he would help me go to the bar when I'd finished my studies. For my part, I was in awe of his ability to negotiate, mitigate and represent.

I was really looking forward to announcing to Lyndon that I would be setting up my own business, but I didn't want to tell him until all the set-up was complete, so Joe and I worked nights and weekends getting the preparatory work done, and I said nothing to Lyndon.

I didn't approach Lyndon until Joe and I had registered our business, found an office and even started hiring staff.

When I announced my news, Lyndon's response was not what I'd expected. In fact, you rarely see a response so far away from what was expected outside of a cheesy situation comedy.

Lyndon was angry, and as he explained why, I became more and more furious with myself. Of course he wasn't going to be happy for me.

'Why didn't you tell me when you first started thinking about this stuff?'

'Because I wanted it to be a surprise?'

'A surprise? Deng, I'm trying to run a business here. You think businesses like surprises like this?'

I hadn't, even for a moment, entertained the possibility of Lyndon being upset, but now I can't believe I'd been so stupid. Of course he and LN Legal weren't simply there to help me achieve my goals. That was a fact that I completely missed.

I'd had to work so hard to get where I was, I had sometimes missed the fact that everybody else struggled too. It was an important realisation. Nobody gave Lyndon anything, and to suggest that he should be happy for me when my triumphs would adversely affect his business – a business that paid me no less – was absurd. That was something that I recognised too late.

I apologised emphatically, but the damage was done. Lyndon forgave me, and even sent some business to AC Law Group, but his wife didn't forgive so quickly. I can understand both decisions.

After leaving LN Legal I had some of the busiest months of my life. I didn't want to cease any of my activities, but it was necessary while Joe and I set up our law firm. I couldn't keep up with two postgraduate courses, pro bono work and my paid work, so I quit the UNSW master's.

•

All the while, back in South Sudan, the pot of discontent was bubbling, fit to spill into war. My conversations with John were never explicit in regards to politics and military machinations – as we all suspected that the CID, South Sudan's secret police, was listening to many of his conversations – but even in his vanilla explanations of what was happening, I could glean the stress and pressure of upcoming conflict.

The stress for John rose when Elizabeth turned up in Juba in September 2013, calling for John and some of his family members to meet with her and her family so their marriage could be traditionally and permanently dissolved.

They all assembled in a large meeting room in Juba, with John and his representatives on one side, and Elizabeth and hers on the other. Elizabeth spoke first, explaining why she thought she should be granted the dissolution. She said that John fulfilled none of the obligations of a husband, and very few of those of a father. Elizabeth explained that both she and John had had children to other people, and said that she was a wife in name only. She said that her dowry, which was to have been thirty-six cows, had never been paid.

Her argument was compelling. John, normally an excellent negotiator, responded only with this:

'I want you back.'

He didn't respond to any of Elizabeth's claims, because they were all true. He just simply, plaintively, asked for her to come back to him. He didn't specify whether that was to happen in South Sudan or Australia, or even if he meant that he wanted to be physically with her. Elizabeth didn't respond to John's pleas, instead she just left. The divorce was approved.

Elizabeth told me later that she both loved and hated John, often at the same time. He was the love of her life, but the source of her greatest disappointment and nothing had ever hurt her like his love affair with her cousin. I didn't speak to John about it afterwards. John wouldn't speak of his heartbreaks any more than he did his triumphs, but the fact that he stood up in front of his family and said he wanted to keep a wife who had borne children from another man spoke to how deep his feelings were for Elizabeth.

The three months after the divorce was a time of tumult, for both John and South Sudan.

The tectonic plates of the SPLA factions were once again straining against each other, ready to rupture. Since independence, President Salva Kiir, a Dinka man, had moved nimbly to consolidate his power in Juba, without unduly slighting the powerful tribal leaders who had the ability to challenge his supremacy. That changed in July, when Kiir dismissed Nuer leader and vice-president Riek Machar, who had previously publicly stated that he would be challenging Kiir for the presidency. Machar made veiled threats, again publicly, while arming and mobilising his militia. The killing finally started in December 2013, when Machar and a group of powerful figures supporting him boycotted a meeting of the National Liberation Council, the country's main legislative organ.

Kiir suspected a coup, so he acted instantly, ordering the largest military unit in Juba – the presidential unit known as the Tiger Battalion – to be disarmed. Shortly after that order, another came, calling for the Dinka soldiers from that unit to be re-armed, ready to be sent into Juba's streets.

After seeing this re-armament, the Nuer officers took their arms up again and a fight started in battalion headquarters. The Dinka troops prevailed, and when they had killed all the Nuer in the base, they went out into the capital and started killing Nuer civilians.

Riek Machar disappeared from the capital, and started adding Nuer deserters to his force of militiamen. Machar also called for the reconstitution of the White Army, his personal massacre machine.

When I heard what was happening in South Sudan, I had panicked thoughts of John and my mother, and Bor and my village. I knew that Bor would likely be the target of revenge for the Nuer, and I thought about how lucky my mother was to have survived the 1991 massacre. I knew also that there would be scant military help in Bor from Salva Kiir. The defence of Juba would be paramount, and Bor would be largely left to its own devices. I also knew that John had sworn that he would never leave Bor defenceless again.

I had to move my mother. Our village would be right in the firing line once again, and I knew it wouldn't be military-aged males who would be targeted. I sent messages and money to my family in Bor, asking for my mother to be escorted to Juba, where I had arranged for her to pick up some money and an air ticket to Uganda.

When I spoke to John, he was as incensed and animated as I'd feared he would be. I thought he might be concerned about his businesses, but it was only his family and his tribe that he was worried about.

Assuming that the CID was now busy and no longer concerned about his conversations, he spoke freely to me about what was happening. He too was convinced that an attack by the White Army was coming, and he was adamant that he would be part of the defence of our villages.

'Not again, not again,' he kept repeating. 'Not again.'

John had been fighting around Juba in 1991 when the Nuer and the White Army attacked. The Dinka had mounted a defence of Bor, but it was too insipid to stop a wholesale massacre. John had always said that his greatest regret in life was that he wasn't present for the defence of Bor.

Not again.

He told me he was going to head north as soon as he could. I wanted my family to be in the safest areas during the upcoming fighting, but I knew there would be no talking John down.

The attack on my homeland finally happened on Wednesday 18 December. By the next day Nuer militia were in control of Bor town, with unfettered access to the undefended villages nearby. A Dinka-dominated counter-offensive was arranged, and by Christmas the Nuer militia were turned back.

Dinka-Bor reservists who could get to Bor did so, including John, who took a platoon of soldiers with him. No one knew when or where the next Nuer attack would come, but there was no doubt that it was coming.

I spoke to John many times a day in that period, when I could raise him. He had little to tell me, only giving me sparse, tactical information with no emotional inflection. He was a soldier again, and had little time for niceties. He would always send love to his children, though.

Even though the counterattack was expected, it also managed to come as a surprise. A few days earlier Nuer fighters had attacked a United Nations base in Akobo, which was close to the Ethiopian border and deep in Nuer territory. The Indian peacekeepers at that base returned fire, but they were just a few dozen against hundreds, and could not repel the attack. More than thirty Dinka people were killed, as well as two peacekeepers.

Unbeknownst to John and those defending Bor, the Nuer had seized a number of large CAT trucks and armoured personnel carriers with UN markings. When they came to Bor, they came disguised, and by the time they started attacking, the defenders were in disarray.

The general retreat was sounded at 10 p.m., and John and his platoon were sent to a village called Goi, and then were ordered back to Juba. John arrived back in the capital, after a brief verbal altercation with the soldiers around the capital who had orders not to let anyone into Juba if they were bearing arms.

In Juba, John briefly met with our mother. She was sick of running, and sick of being in strange places, so she had come back to South Sudan under her own steam. She said that whatever her fate was, it was in her village. John said he felt roughly the same way.

High-ranking SPLA officials who had John's best interests in mind told my brother not to go back to Bor and, in fact, explicitly ordered him not to, even posting men in the lobby of the building he was staying in to make sure he didn't try to go back.

John called me on his way to Bor. He had broken a window to escape, and had found a vehicle. He was heading north on his own.

'I said "never again" and I meant it,' he said to me, when I implored him to turn back.

The next time I spoke to him, he had been shot. John had found a Dinka SPLA unit in a village called Pariek, very close to Malek. There the unit had engaged with the Nuer militiamen and John had been shot through the back while fighting. He was okay, though. He had been shot before, and he knew this was not a fatal wound. I urged caution. What else could I do? He said he would be as careful as he could be. What else could he do?

I lost contact with John after that. The Nuer pushed on, and carved through the Dinka units, like the one John had been fighting with. Their advance towards Juba was only stopped when Salva Kiir called on Uganda to mobilise helicopter gunships, which decimated the rebel heavy-armoured vehicles that were surging towards the capital.

John's phone was dead, and I couldn't raise anyone who he would have been in contact with. I called everyone I could who might know where he might be and eventually word of his whereabouts made its way back to me. A lot of the wounded Dinka soldiers had been evacuated across the Nile to the marshy banks on the other side. John was one of those wounded. To know that he was across the river, and being guarded by the Dinka-Aliab who had looked after my mother before, was a huge relief.

I waited a day for news from John, and then another. There was no news. I called John many times, but each time his phone was dead. I phoned everyone else I knew in South Sudan, but they couldn't help. No one knew what had happened to him.

Then I got a call at work from a man named Ajok Kuol Ajok, someone of great standing in our Sudanese community in Sydney. As soon as I heard his voice, my stomach fell to my feet and then it fissured and died when he said he needed to meet me face to face. For us Dinka it's always someone greatly respected who delivers the worst of news, and that news is always delivered in person. I asked Ajok what he wanted. He said he couldn't speak to me about it on the phone.

I knew then that John was dead. Earlier that day, my other brother Akau in South Sudan had said he would try to find out what had happened to John. If he had found John alive, I would have received a phone call from South Sudan, not from Sydney.

I was no longer panicked, but the colour of life faded and all the sound muted. I could not smell or taste. When I met with Ajok and he told me that John was dead, it was as though I was watching the scene on a small screen. I was not even there. I was angry and sad and curious, but all those emotions were writ small, because mostly I was numb.

I thought about Elizabeth and the children. I would have to tell them – that is the way of things for us. It would be my responsibility. I would have people with me when I did, but I would have to tell them. I would be telling them that John was dead. John was dead. John was dead.

It was a strange thought to think. John was dead. So many had died, but they had not been John. They couldn't have been John, but now he was in their number.

I went home from work and sat quietly. I didn't cry – over the years I had become immune to that particular response to death – but I was shaken to the core.

People died, randomly, violently and without warning, I knew that better than anyone. Both John and I had known that when he returned to South Sudan he was putting himself in extreme danger, doubly so when he ran towards the front lines of the emerging civil war, but for John to be dead? It felt like an affront against nature.

John had seemed an irresistible force. Despite being shot and blown up, despite being dropped in the middle of a strange nation, despite being passed over for all the jobs he wanted and deserved, despite his marriage dissolving, John always persevered, and at the end, he even thrived.

John was dead. It was as if the wind had forever stopped blowing, or the sky had become forever black.

I couldn't tell Elizabeth or the kids that day. I just sat in my apartment and stared at the wall throughout the afternoon and night. I did not sleep.

Early in the morning I spoke to Akau, who had found John's body. The deathblow had been a single round in the back of the head.

In the morning I visited Elizabeth and the children, with a huge contingent of family and community. Their world was similarly devastated. Elizabeth's face turned and contorted when I told her the news. She had always loved John despite their endless and existential differences. This was the end of that love.

In the coming weeks I took on the grief that the death of a brother brings, but also grief for the crushing sadness of John's fate. John had done everything an uneducated African soldier in the maddest of wars could do to escape his circumstances. He received the thunderbolt of luck that was needed too. He was as smart as a professor, as engaging as a statesman and as driven as a billionaire, and his life ended prematurely, thousands of kilometres from his children, his love and his brother.

I kept seeing my brother's dead body in my mind. I saw the dried blood, and the gouge of the wound – the empty expression and the dirty clothes. He looked like litter in my mind, because dead people on the battlefield always looked like litter, except if you recognised the dead and remembered when they loved and were loved in return.

Chapter Nine

A SON OF SYDNEY

I thought a lot about identity after John died. I realised that one of the great differences between John and me was that John would say that he was South Sudanese, and I would say I was Australian.

John had always been a pragmatist while I was an idealist. It was his pragmatism that bound him to South Sudan, and my idealism was the reason John said I should avoid our homeland. One thing that we shared was that we were drawn to South Sudan, in a very elemental way. I loved the country, the Nile, the people, and our identity as Dinka, as did John. I will always be tied to the land of my birth while my mother is still alive in that country.

After John's death, I wondered again if my future lay in South Sudan, but I realised that my life was, and would continue to be, in Australia. My friends were in Australia, my outlook on life was Australian, and so my career and future were also in Australia.

I am driven by justice and there is a surmountable amount of inequality and injustice in Australia. That's not true of South Sudan. When John died, I knew instantly that there was no chance of bringing my brother's killers to justice, nor was there even much chance of discovering who was responsible. Could you ever say the same of a murder in Australia?

I knew also there was little likelihood of John's assets being settled fairly. John had died a very successful South Sudanese businessman, and while I couldn't decide if that fact mitigated the sadness or amplified it, it certainly complicated things. It's possible that John died with more than a million dollars (and possibly close to two) in assets, and I hoped that Elizabeth and the children would benefit from that.

I told Elizabeth that she should travel to South Sudan and pursue John's assets. I helped arrange legal representation for her, but when she and Joshua arrived in Juba, she received a hostile reception. Some cousins of ours had assumed control of John's house and his businesses, and she also found that they had the patronage to ensure that no court would change the state of affairs. She returned to Sydney in no better position than when she'd left.

For my part, I disappeared into my work after John's death. I started to wonder what life was all about – life in general, and also mine and John's. What was John's life about? John eventually found the success and money he yearned for, but was never able to share it with his children or the woman he shared so much with previously. Was John's life about those moments of hope, like when he first met Joshua, or when we received our Australian visas, or when he graduated from university – the first Sudanese man to do so in Australia – or when I graduated from law school?

John did so much for me. I calmed myself in the belief that John's life had been about the service of his community, and in the service of people like me. I never thanked John for bringing me to Australia and raising me. He didn't do it for thanks, but I still deeply wish I had said something – anything – that sounded like appreciation. John did a great deal for South Sudan, and for Bor. I decided that I should contribute to my community also, but my community was Western Sydney, and especially the African diaspora around me.

I increased the amount of pro bono work I did, and also made myself available for media engagements. There had been some interest in John's story over the years, and his studies had partially been subsidised by telling the story of how Christine brought us to Australia in some magazines. There had been talk of John writing a book some years ago too, but that idea died when he returned to South Sudan. John's story was an exceptional one in Australia, but his injuries and heartbreaks were of the garden variety in East Africa.

I believed more and more in the importance of telling the refugee story, specifically the African refugee story in Australia. That would be my weapon against the tribalism and prejudice I hated so much. An old axiom is that to know someone is to love someone. If people knew what huge efforts people like John had undertaken to live a life so many take for granted in a place like Australia, perhaps they would be more understanding of our different appearance or manner. I thought that was important work.

In 2012 I was part of a few SBS programs. The first, called 'Trained to Kill' on *Insight*, looked at what's required to train someone to take a life, and also about how that affects that person mentally for the rest of their lives.

Studies have proven that it is generally unusual for a human being to be able to kill another human without great provocation or training. In fact, a great deal of modern military training is essentially designed to override the protocols and safeguards in almost all of us that make it difficult for a human to willingly and knowingly take a life.

It seems that those protocols and safeguards are ill-formed when we are children, and that is part of the reason that my prepubescent friends and I were called to prosecute the war in Sudan. But child soldiers must continue fighting and killing throughout their lives, or they will have moments where the mad morality of their childhood will rage against their adult self's moral reasoning, causing dangerous mental fissures.

I had been trained to kill, and I had helped contribute to the death of Didinga tribespeople. When I was a boy, I had been able to put the visions of their melting faces aside because that atrocity had happened in a time and place of endless violence. The Didinga had died, others had died, and I thought most likely I would die, so the details of their deaths disappeared into the background noise of the war.

I hadn't taken on the weight of those deaths in Sudan, because there was no suggestion that I should feel the shame of their murder. In Australia – living a normal Australian life and championing fairness and justice – I knew that I had been involved in an outrage. I had been a child when it had happened, and I knew intellectually there was nothing I could have done to stop it, but I had been involved. I raged against police and court inequities, but I never came up against any transgression that was as outrageous as the one that I had been complicit in.

I still have nightmares about Kapoeta, but increasingly in my sleep I am in a bush camp, watching people wriggle and squirm as they are being tortured, and sometimes I am watching their skin bubble and burst as flames lick their bodies.

I suppose the nightmares where I'm in Kapoeta are mostly about existentialism, but the nightmares with the Didinga people are about community. What did I owe those tribespeople? So much more than what I blithely and willingly gave them. I think perhaps the torture and murder dreams are a reminder that I owe a debt to the world that I can never repay, but must forever try to.

I was part of another episode of *Insight* that was looking at the rites of passage, and ideas of manhood. I told my story and explained how I would not be considered a man in my culture because I never completed the appropriate rituals. I hadn't really articulated that fact before and so the strangeness of it hadn't really occurred to me, although I had felt the lack of it.

It is a strange fact, though, that war could make one less of a man. It's contrary to historical conventional wisdom, especially in a country that has been defined by war for so long.

After appearing on *Insight*, I was disoriented. I was somewhat bolstered by the realisation that Dinka culture was separate from the militarisation of the country, but it still bothered me that I was set apart from my tribesmen who had gone through the rituals of manhood.

I was in the same boat as many South Sudanese men my age though, and the tribal rules had not been relaxed. I could not marry traditionally, and people considered me differently when they knew I had not been through the rituals. If I were to have a son, then he would be subject to the greatest insult one might level in South Sudan – someone may call him the 'son of a boy'.

This insult is usually met with violence.

But then again, what did I care? I'm an Australian, living in Australia, where I am considered a man. There are some fluid definitions of manhood in Australia, but generally you are a boy for seventeen years and 364 days and then, the next day, you're a man: too easy. There would be no Australians who wouldn't consider me a man, no woman who would refuse my hand because she and her family saw me as a six-foot, seventy-five kilogram boy.

I had always abstractly assumed that I would go back and fulfil the rituals at some point, but after my appearance on *Insight*, I started to wonder if I ever would. I also started to think a lot about whom I owed fealty to. I owed a lot to the Catholics, but couldn't really dedicate myself to them, as I never believed in their god, and way of life. Their dedication to compassion and justice I believed in, but dogmatism is something I really despise.

I do owe a debt to the continent of my birth, because my skin is built for their sun, and my soul is made of East African soil. I don't owe a debt to the countries though, and I certainly feel no debt to the SPLA. I realised I owe a debt to the African people, and especially those Africans in Sydney who helped me feel comfortable in a strange city. And I owe a debt to Western Sydney for giving me a community, especially Western Sydney University.

Law is now my life, in a way that soldiering once was.

That thought was forefront when, in 2013, I was contacted by a representative of the university who was asking if I'd like to be involved in an advertisement. Of course I was happy to help.

The advertisement was to be a short explanation of how I made my way from my village in rural Sudan to a court in Sydney with, of course, a strong focus on the university's involvement.

One day I sat down with the director and we spoke about my journey, and a few months later we were shooting.

When I saw the finished product, I was very happy. The advertisement was short, but emotional, and true. I especially liked the music from Brisbane singer Jarryd James. Another thing I liked about the advertisement was how many South Sudanese were employed as extras. I still have people coming up to me telling me that they got a day's work as a soldier, or villager.

I really had no conception of how popular the advertisement would end up being, nor the doors it would open for me. The advertisement went viral the day it went up on YouTube, and soon my Facebook feed was clogged with people sharing it. That day my phone rang literally every few seconds – usually friends and colleagues calling either to offer congratulations, or to ask about the veracity of the advertisement.

The advertisement kept bouncing around the world, and there were tens of thousands of views in a few hours, then hundreds of thousands after weeks, and then millions after months. It was an artful piece of work, but I found the interest a little confounding.

There was a perception that my story was exceptional, but I didn't think that was true. I had been marched for a month as a child, but everyone had. I had been trained in a military camp, but everyone had. I fought as everyone had, I was injured as everyone was and I had suffered, as everyone had. I survived, but not everyone had, although enough had for it not to be of interest. A lot of those who had survived thrived, also. I was in contact with a lot of people who I'd fought with – usually connecting on Facebook – and many of the surviving boys have gained educations and made something of themselves: some in South Sudan, and many in places like Canada, the US, the UK and France. In fact, in many ways my story is far less interesting than John's.

'Why me?' I asked myself.

I realised that I was asking the wrong question. It didn't matter why it was me who was garnering all that interest, I should be asking what I could do with it.

After the advertisement started to gain momentum, Western Sydney University decided to set up a half million-dollar scholarship for refugee students, and I joined the advisory panel. I felt obliged to do as much as I could to tell my story, and promote refugee awareness and acceptance.

I wanted to explain the circumstances that had brought us to Australia, and tell people how hard life had been when we came here. I wanted people to understand that no one ever wants to be a refugee. I wanted to explain that we had taken public money in the early days of our resettlement, but that there was no other way to get on our feet, and that once we did we contributed. I wanted to champion Dinka culture, and also explain that I believed that tribalism was one of the world's great pitfalls – contradictory as those thoughts were.

Although I wasn't thinking it consciously, and rarely had his name in my mouth, I wanted to tell John's story, too. Perhaps I was trying to speak to the people who'd received John's CV, and sat across from him in job interviews at the start of his career, who were confused by him and his African-ness. If only they'd understood how hard a worker he was, how bright and driven he was, then maybe he wouldn't have left Australia, and maybe he would still be alive.

I started taking on extra speaking engagements – at business conferences, or with individual high schoolers, all anyone needed to do was to explain how I might be able to help them and I would agree to speak.

My law business saw only a small increase in clients when the Western Sydney University advertisement spread, but as I took on more and more of these speaking engagements, more and more people with legal quandaries came through our door. I had made a commitment to Joe and the business, and a commitment to myself to continue my pro bono work, and I was speaking whenever I could, so my life was consumed by those obligations and I was working most hours of every day.

I waited for the burnout, but it never came. I didn't tire of criminal defence, nor did I grow tired of my desire for advocacy for refugee visibility and understanding. I still don't tire of it.

I'm sure there are many wise men and women who say that it's unhealthy for a human mind and body to be in perpetual motion, and furthermore I can imagine that some people would say that endless work is an attempt to silence the fearful things that lie in the quiet, still moments. I'm sure they are right, too, but this works for me.

My days are full now – all of them – with endeavours I deem worthwhile, and that's all I want from my life. It's what I owe and what I've earned.

Then near the end of 2015, I was invited to make a speech I wasn't willing to give. The invitation came in the mail, sent from the office of The Honourable Mike Baird, Premier of New South Wales.

It was a personal letter from the premier, asking me to consider giving the Australia Day address at the New South Wales Conservatorium of Music. Furthermore, he said the address would be reprinted in the *Sydney Morning Herald*, and would be shown, in its entirety on the public broadcaster, the ABC.

I went to the Australia Day website and saw the men and women who had previously given the address. They were people who had dedicated their whole lives to the service of others and also people who towered in the legal profession – judges and justices.

I was an infant in law – a solicitor with a small criminal practice, and a Blacktown boy who liked to tell the story of how he came to Australia. I wanted to tell my story, but I felt I was truly unworthy. There was a small part of me that suspected the letter was a hoax, and a larger, more fearful part of me that knew it wasn't.

I knew if I ever began a correspondence with the premier, he would convince me – I thought him quite a charming man – and I truly felt he had made a mistake asking me to give this address, so I ignored the letter.

I went about my business and a couple of weeks later another letter came from the premier, once again from Premier Baird himself, and once again asking me to consider speaking on Australia Day.

I felt only fear when I held that letter. I asked a colleague of mine, Jessica, to call the premier's office and find out if the letter had actually come from Premier Baird. The bad news came; the letter did truly come from him.

I really didn't want to give the speech, but I realised I couldn't just ignore the request away either. I spent a good part of a day speaking to the people I respected the most. They uniformly said that I should take up the offer to speak.

The most compelling of those voices was that of Hugh Selby, a barrister of incomparable intelligence and a man who has been my mentor since he supervised my master's thesis.

Hugh's argument was impeccable – as all of Hugh's arguments are – explaining to me that neither humility nor humiliation should ever stop someone from speaking a helpful truth.

Hugh's words compelled me, but what actually put me over the line was an opinion that was silent – an opinion I wanted, but would never have again.

I wanted to ask John what he thought I should do.

I called the premier's office and told them I would give the address, but I will admit that I called that office a few times in the following weeks, telling them that if they found someone more appropriate, I would be happy for them to replace me. They told me the same thing each time – Premier Baird very much wanted me to speak.

There was no getting out of it. I sat at my desk one afternoon – after my last call to the premier's office – and I mused about what I would actually speak about. I had some stump speeches in my pocket – mostly biographical with no inflection or judgement, just what was inherent in the facts – but as I thought more about the opportunity, it occurred to me that I really wanted to speak about what Australia meant to me, and what it had meant to John.

I was far from being the traditional, parochial Australian patriot, but I believed in the opportunities and freedom that had been afforded me in this country. I also understood the cultural limitations of those opportunities and freedoms.

I wanted those beliefs and understandings represented in my speech. I wanted to challenge the senior Crown prosecutor who once told me that I didn't look like an 'ordinary Australian' in an open courtroom.

I believed – and still believe – in Australia's commitment to fairness and equality but, even so, I understood it isn't as easy being a black Australian as it could be: as it should be. Change can happen in places like Australia – we have the appropriate conditions. In Australia we have usable courts, and elected leaders, and there is no famine or debilitating war or economic crisis (despite what we are sometimes told). There is no reason, as Australians, not to be our most inclusive, most compassionate selves.

There will always be voices saying that Australia can't financially or culturally afford to welcome those in distress. There will always be fearmongering too, and commentators who choose to compare all dark-skinned people to the worst examples of their genetic brethren. To offset those voices, we need examples of simple, comparative humanity, so I also thought my speech should be personal and biographical.

Slowly but surely the speech started to take shape, and when I had a first draft I approached a man whose opinions I respected greatly – Justice Terry Buddin. Justice Buddin was one of my professors at the University of Wollongong, and not only would he give me a sense of whether my feelings and attitudes were represented in the text, but he would also be able to give comment on the performance aspect of such a speech.

After reading the speech to him, Justice Buddin told me that the script needed no rewrite, but he did stress that I should give the speech in the mirror repeatedly while timing myself, to make sure that there would be no part of it that would make me stumble, and also to make sure I wouldn't drag or rush the speech.

Justice Buddin also stressed that I should visit the auditorium before I gave the speech. To this day I have no idea if it was wise advice, or debilitating counsel.

When I walked into Verbrugghen Hall, the main auditorium at the Sydney Conservatorium of Music, I was instantly and completely overawed by the place. It was the largest auditorium I'd spoken in, but more than that, it seemed a place of august countenance. From the giant organ on the stage, to its location, nestled inside Sydney's Royal Botanical Gardens, the hall spoke of Australia's grand anglicised past and, in contrast, I could only think of my own humble African past. When I stepped into that hall I was a dirty, scared, mute boy again, worth nothing and surely destined for nothing.

In the days leading up to the speech I was convinced I was going to finish talking and people would respond with a collective response of 'who cares?'. The premier would come and give me a consolation pat on the back, and I would say to him: 'I tried to tell you.'

The day I was to give the speech, I became quite ill with the flu. Aside from the illnesses I suffered in Sudan – and possibly because of them – I almost never get sick, but when I woke that day every part of my body ached. My mind didn't want to give that damn speech, and now my body didn't want to either. A few cups of coffee later, though, I was in front of a lectern, facing hundreds of people with the unblinking eyes of a bank of cameras behind them.

I hadn't been that nervous since I faced fire back in Sudan. I only remember starting the speech, and then I went into autopilot. Here is an edited transcript:

Firstly, I would like to acknowledge the traditional owners of this land, past and present, the Gadigal people of the Eora nation.

Ten years ago, Clover Moore, the lord mayor of Sydney, talked at the National Maritime Museum. She said, 'Today, as we mark the beginning of Refugee Week, it is important to remember that all non-Indigenous Australians are immigrants to this land.'

She continued, 'From the perspective of thousands of years of Aboriginal custodianship, the rest of us are newcomers.' I wonder what the Gadigal people in 1788 thought as they watched sailing ships coming up their harbour? Did they realise that their civilisation was about to be uprooted? Did they watch with interest and wonder? How soon did that interest turn to mortal fear?

It has been a 200-year journey for their descendants to reassert the right to be free of those fears, to acclaim pride in their traditions. That's a long wait.

The theme of this year's Australia Day address is that freedom from fear is very special to all of us. To appreciate the value of freedom one must first be denied it. To know real fear gives special meaning and yearning to being free of fear.

So what does 'freedom from fear' entail for you and me as Australians, or those who 'want to be Australians' in 2016? Let me share with you parts of my story. It may be unfamiliar to those who have been born and grown up in a peaceful Australia. To those who have come as refugees from the world's trouble spots, parts of this story will be too familiar. A point of this story is to emphasise how very lucky we are to enjoy freedom from fear, and how very unlucky are many, many others who neither choose, nor deserve their fate.

I was born in a small fishing village called Malek, in the South Sudan. My father was a fisherman and we had a banana farm. I am one of eight children born to Mr Thiak Adut Garang and Ms Athieu Akau Deng. So the parts of my name are drawn from both my parents. My given name is Deng which means 'god of the rain'. In those parts of this wide brown land that are short of water my name might be a good omen. I have a nickname: *Aolouch*, which means 'swallow'. Alas, I couldn't fly and as a young boy, about the age of a typical second grader in Sydney, I was conscripted into an army.

As they took me away from my home and family, I didn't even understand what freedoms I had lost. I didn't understand how fearful I should have been. I was young. I was ignorant. I lost the freedom to read and write. I lost the freedom to sing children's songs. I lost the right to be innocent. I lost the right to be a child.

Instead, I was taught to sing war songs. In place of the love of life I was taught to love the death of others.

I had one freedom – the freedom to die, and I'll return to that a little later.

I lost the right to say what I thought. In place of 'free speech', I was an oppressor to those who wanted to express opinions that were different to those who armed me, fed me, told me what to think, where to go and what to do.

And there was something else very special to me that was taken away. I was denied the right to become an initiated member of my tribe. The mark of 'inclusiveness' was denied to me. I had to wait until I became an Australian citizen to know that I belonged.

As an Australian I am proud that we have a national anthem. It's ours and to hear it played and sung is to feel pride, pride that we are a nation of free people. It has a historical background that is familiar to those who grew up here, but which is not easily understood by newcomers. I found it useful to take some lines from our anthem to bring together what I want to share with you.

To be here today, talking about freedom from fear, about the rewards that come from thinking 'inclusively', rather than thinking 'divisively', is to achieve something that the child conscript Deng could not imagine.

I came to Australia as an illiterate, penniless teenager, traumatised physically and emotionally by war. In Sudan,

I was considered legally disabled, only by virtue of being black or having a dark skin complexion. As you can see I am very black and proud of my dark skin complexion. But in the Sudan my colour meant that my prospects could go no further than a dream of being allowed to finish a primary education. To be a lawyer was unthinkable.

Australia opened the doors of its schools and universities. I would particularly like to thank the Western Sydney University where I received my law degree and the University of Wollongong where I obtained my Master's degree in Law – an experience which enabled me to realise my dream of becoming a court room advocate. Australia educated me. How lucky I became. How lucky is any person who receives an education in a free land and goes on to use it in daily life.

I was among many young children forcibly removed from their homes and families and marched to Ethiopia, for reasons that were unknown to me at the time. I walked thousands of kilometres without shoes or underwear.

What do we take for granted as Australians? Free education, food, clothing (more than shoes and under-wear), shelter, healthcare and personal safety. We take those things for granted until we don't have them.

I witnessed children like myself dying as we made our way, barefoot and starving. As a child, witnessing the death of a relative is something that stays with you for life. Even today, I remember the deadened face and the gaunt skeletal body of one of my cousins lying on a corn sack. I saw too much abuse and death among my friends during the war. I sustained physical abuse from my superiors because of my inability to follow orders and for demanding decent treatment. I was a child soldier and I was expected to kill or be killed.

Within a year, I was plagued by disease and malnutrition. I felt isolated and deserted. I remember being told off by one of my close relatives because I was poking him with my protruding bones. He too was a forced conscript. We were stationed in a camp in Western Ethiopia that was disguised as though it was a refugees' camp. He told me I should just die. I understand now that he too was suffering from depression and by caring for me he was unable to improve his own situation. By this time, I could only take fluids. I feel sorry for my relative. I do not believe that he was trying to be cruel. He was just a child too, unable to properly look after me or himself.

In those days, what I needed was a loving parent. What child, taken away from the care of his or her parents, will not suffer some form of psychological trauma? What child, merely seven years of age and ordered to witness deaths by firing squads, will not suffer a lasting injury?

What child, upon seeing dead bodies, lying in pools of moving blood, will not suffer some sort of long-term psychological damage?

Around 1993, I watched some boys, only ten or eleven years old, as they picked up their AK-47s, put the gun to their heads, squeezed the trigger with their own fingers and blew out their brains. In a better world, those fingers might have made music in a place such as this hall, built homes, operated the equipment of scientific discovery. Instead their short lives were as nothing – innocents destroyed. I, consumed by fear, couldn't pull a trigger myself, because I was too scared. Yes, fear saved me. But I understand why they did it. For my fellow child soldiers, pulling the trigger was the quickest way to die and for them the thought of dying was better than the reality of living.

I wonder what their spirits would have thought if they saw that I would become a practising lawyer in Australia some eighteen years later. I grieve for them. For them, the freedom from fear was death. I was lucky. You are too. Freedom from fear is about acceptance of our common identity. For we Australians in 2016 freedom from fear is almost taken for granted. We had better take care to keep it.

Let me turn now from memories of death to messages of hope, first for new arrivals to these shores and then to those who have long called Australia home.

To those recently arrived, do not give up the dream that brought you here. Within every Australian community there are people who were immigrants or whose parents were immigrants. Treat the experiences that brought you here as tough training for the journey of establishing new lives, new families, new careers.

Clover Moore, in that same speech I mentioned earlier, noted that, 'The Australian national anthem has promised that, for those who've come across the sea, we've boundless plains to share.' Surprise! Surprise! Australia is a nation where most of us, most of the time, seek to give and receive a 'fair go' and 'respect democracy'. It's that 'fair go' that you see in every new Australian success story. That is the 'Advance Australia Fair' in the anthem.

I know that some who are watching and listening will be wondering why I, so black, am ignoring that the ruling majority appear to be white. I don't ignore it, just as I don't ignore that the colours and faces of the Australian community are such a rich palette. Take a trip around an Australian city, visit a building site, walk around an educational campus, look at the names in our sporting teams, and hear, see, smell and taste the richness of the cultures in any of our shopping centres. White is a colour to which so much can be added.

I remind every youthful migrant to remember and cherish where you came from. It is your grounding, just as important to you as this land is to the traditional owners of this place. Your parents and relatives made sacrifices for your freedom to be here without fear. You must have a dream that takes you up and beyond any past trauma and turmoil. We are special, each and every one of us. You are special to this nation and you ought to listen to your heart and take hold of opportunities.

Of course fears arrive unbidden and unwelcome. We all experience that from time to time. Can we get and keep a job? How do we keep our cherished cultural traditions alive? Can we earn respect? Will we be listened to? But don't fight your fears alone. Here we have the freedom to seek help from new friends, the elders, even a stranger who can be your friend at the time you need them. Remember, fellow immigrants, we begin as strangers in this land and we have much to learn. But the freedoms of this place mean that most of the time, from most people, there is a welcoming hand. So fear not.

That leads me to those who are settled Australians. These past few years there have been unexpected fears, the fears that random atrocities such as those that took place in Bali, and more recently in London, Paris and Istanbul, will come here. We scarcely notice the frequency of such acts in other places where terror, not freedom from fear, is the norm.

Fears and doubt are the ideal environment in which to breed misguided obsessions and grand delusions. There is nothing new in such manipulation. It was done to me. Such manipulation of the confused and searching spirit of youth is essential for those who use others in their quest for power.

In responding to tragedies in which the lives of victims and perpetrators alike have been snuffed out to serve some demagogue, we must all be careful not to let local opportunists exploit our emotions with simplistic solutions.

What seems new for us Australians is that the physical barriers to terror, such as distance and sea, are now irrelevant. But this is just the shortness of memory. These barriers became irrelevant for the traditional owners of this land when the winds and the currents brought the ships of the First Fleet up this harbour. More recently these barriers were no barriers at all when midget submarines entered Sydney Harbour during the Second World War.

Then, as now, freedom from fear is something that must be fought for. It can never be taken for granted. Fighting must sometimes be physical and our war memorials are testament to those who fought and gave their all. But the first line of defence against consuming fear is always our collective hearts and minds.

And collectively what makes this nation one to be proud of is the willingness of most in our communities to be accepting, tolerant, inclusive and welcoming. Our anthem speaks of the courage needed to let us all combine. Now is the time.

The fears among us are not limited to terrorism. It is all too clear that partner abuse and child abuse flourished in families where the victims were afraid to speak out. It is not so long ago that gays and lesbians lived in fear of exposure. Attitudes and actions needed to change and that has happened, but there is still more to be done.

This afternoon, I delight in thanking all those whose support for 'freedom from fear' never wavers. These are the people, the people all around us, who freely gave me hope and sustained it. They understand the journey that has brought new arrivals to these shores from war, famine, oppression, and which then becomes the new journey that follows a new path, a path of 'freedom from fear'.

The spirit of giving walks that same path to remind us all about the less fortunate. The reward of freedom from fear has a price: to willingly give for others without hope of anything beyond 'thanks'. This is an obligation that never ends.

One of my early Australian friends illustrates this point. He bought me my first bicycle and got me a job to mow lawns. Geoff died a decade ago, and I shall always remember him for his encouragement, his faith and his investment in me.

There are now so many friends, colleagues and teachers who all in different ways have led me here. I thank you all, not only for your help to me but the likely help you have given others too.

Last but not least, my gratitude is to fellow Australians for opening the door, not only to me but to all the other migrants like me. Without your spirit of a fair go, my story could not have been told.

We acquire our community wisdom from our collective, shared experiences.

It's that wisdom which underlies our entitlement to sing in joyful strains how proud we are today to be Australians.

Let's look at the future. My guru told me to live so that I can build a living memorial for my departed loved ones. There will be a charitable foundation in the name of my murdered brother, John Mac. We will raise funds and take action to alleviate poverty, bring education and better health to the lands where I was born and he died.

I will try to follow in the footsteps of a man who wanted to make things right.

I hope that I can be like my friend Geoff, giving less fortunate people a fair go.

I hope that all of us, each in our own way, will strive to understand and help others.

I wish us all a Happy Australia Day.

Whenever I practised the speech, it was around twenty-five minutes. When I actually gave the address, it ran for more than forty minutes. The premier greeted me very warmly and kindly afterwards though, and if he was only giving me platitudes, he gave them expertly. People cried in the auditorium.

That afternoon I went to work, and instantly the speech seemed a distant memory.

The speech was received very well, and I was offered so many new speaking engagements, I had to start picking and choosing. There were other offers too, outside of speaking engagements. A Sydney artist asked me to sit for him so he could paint me for inclusion into the Archibald Prize. After looking at his work, I agreed. After just two sittings – one at my office and another at his studio in St Leonards – he saw deeply into me.

The artist, named Nick Stathopoulos, had asked for some photographs before our meetings, and I sent a collection. When we met, he took some more pictures as we were talking and joking around.

Nick called me a few days later telling me that I didn't look comfortable in any of the photographs, nor when I sat for him. He said he now wanted to capture the questioning, uneasy restlessness that he saw in my face. It was a bold thing to say of someone he barely knew, but he had understood something essential and true of me. Perhaps it was experiences, or perhaps it was my nature, but I am very rarely at peace or at ease, regardless of the situation.

I was impressed with both Nick's insight and his portrait, which artfully represents not only my visage, but also a little bit of my soul. The painting was recognised as a finalist in the Archibald competition, and I am very grateful to Nick for his efforts and his insights.

A number of publishers also approached me to see if I would be interested in writing a memoir. I thought for some time about the offer. Initially I was, once again, reluctant because I was such a young man, and only a relative newcomer to the world of legal representation. It occurred to me, though, that a complete three-act story was behind me – birth to war, war to Australia and Australia to western normalcy. I also very much wanted to write about John, and, sadly, the whole story of his life was written.

As I thought more about it, I was put in the mind of Hugh Selby's words about the relative sizes of humility and the potential benefit of speaking a useful truth.

When I spoke in public, I very much believed in the usefulness of what I spoke about. I knew that people came to hear about war and sadness and a past that was so unusual for them, but I also knew that they left thinking about how normal my present was – and how much I was like them.

My skin was usually much darker than theirs, and my accent is still quite thick, but I am just an Australian, like they are. Speed cameras annoy me, I call people 'mate' when I forget their name, I like pies and schnitzels, and a flat white in the morning, and lager at the end of a warm day. The only real difference between you and me was that I had to fight to become Australian. I thought it important to relate that fact to as many people as possible. If you can relate to me – a reformed child soldier coming from one of the most isolated and disadvantaged nations on earth – then there are few refugees in Australia that you can't relate to. And if you relate to them, you can have compassion for them and their circumstances.

When I signed to do this book, I had one immutable request – my co-author and I would travel back to South Sudan. I wanted the person I would be writing the book with to see the flow of the Nile, and the skin of the people. I wanted them to eat the fresh fish, and speak to my mother and my cousins, and the people I fought with. I also wanted those things for me, and if I was going to write about John's death, I wanted to know what had really happened to him on that final day.

Chapter Ten

THE FINAL RETURN

Before my co-writer, Ben, and I could go to South Sudan, we had to spend a week in the Ethiopian capital Addis Ababa, so Ben could get a South Sudanese visa.

I'd heard of Addis Ababa when I was in Pinyudo. In my mind as a child, though, Addis Ababa was a force and an entity – it ordered and provided things, like a general or a god – and it was only much later that I realised it was also a place.

In the 1990s, Addis Ababa was already a city of millions of people, rushing in and out of huge, multi-storey buildings, dodging Soviet-era and modern Western European vehicles flying along multi-lane roads. If I had visited Addis Ababa as a war boy, the place would have blown my mind. As an adult, it reminded me of how far even the best-performing states in Africa have to go compared to places like Sydney.

As a boy, I would have visited Addis Ababa at the pleasure of the Derg, an ostensibly communist, Soviet-backed military junta that ruled Ethiopia at the time. They were the primary supporters of the SPLA, and the group who facilitated my training in Pinyudo in the Western Ethiopia region. Now I travelled to Ethiopia courtesy of the Ethiopian People's Revolutionary Democratic Front or EPRDF – a group that helped facilitate the attack on my training camp in Pinyudo.

They are, I suppose, my former enemies.

Like most organisations with 'people's' and 'democratic' and 'revolutionary' in their title, they are an authoritarian regime that does not suffer opposition. They are also largely benevolent – relatively progressive, not overly militaristic (for the region) and perhaps a pragmatic example of what we might hope the SPLA could transition into.

I have always liked Ethiopians. Their food is wonderful, their coffee is perhaps the finest in the world, and they are, more often than not, kind and funny. I was very excited to visit Ethiopia as an adult, but from the first night I arrived, I had terrible, vivid dreams.

I saw death that first night. In my dreams I saw the wooden guns and the boys in corn sacks with hollow cheeks, and I saw the Gilo River, swallowing weak bodies while the tiny splashes of machine-gun bullets pierced the water. I saw the Eritrean women exposing their naked bodies, guns slung over their shoulders, and I heard their horrible laughter.

On my second day in Addis Ababa I visited a small, private museum called the Red Terror Museum, which details the rise, reign and fall of the Derg. The museum had an exhibition showing the Derg's favourite torture techniques, which included a particular stress position whereby the subject was hogtied, feet up, so a rhino-skin whip could be lashed across their soles.

The museum's guide explained that this method of torture was developed in the Soviet Union, and made its way to Addis Ababa courtesy of advisors from Russia's secret intelligence and security agencies, the GRU and KGB. It was almost exactly the same way I and the other war boys had flagellated the Didinga people. The facial features of the exhibit's fibreglass man brought back strong visual memories. I saw pleading, and I saw agony, and I saw despair.

Usually in my nightmares I was being hunted, but the night after that visit to the museum, I was the one hunting. One nightmare was no better or worse than the other.

Senior members of the Derg still live among their victims in Addis Ababa, and their leader Mengistu lives a life of luxury as a guest of Robert Mugabe in Zimbabwe. There is no justice in Africa, and that's perhaps the main reason I do not think I could ever live there again.

South Sudan is perhaps the epicentre of African injustice. Criminals, thieves and murderers are dotted around the capital, Juba. They ignore the new traffic lights built with the help of the UN, they eat at expensive restaurants made possible by the *kawaja* economy, they drink Johnnie Walker Black Label (not the Jeanie Waker Black Liable made by local bootleggers) and every day they stuff their offshore bank accounts with more money.

In Addis Ababa I visited the Australian consulate, and an Australian military contact of mine said it best when he said: 'In a place like South Sudan the corruption would be almost understandable, if they just left a little bit for the people . . . if they didn't feel the need to take it all.'

When we landed in Juba Airport, the runways were crammed with giant white helicopters and transport planes from the UN and other NGOs, and the hot, sweaty terminal was full of *kawaja* and other Africans who had come to help in the ongoing efforts of building a nation.

If you only work in one of the barbwire-ringed and air-conditioned compounds, and go from compound to compound, and eat in well-stocked restaurants, and drink ice-cold beers, Juba seems like a city on the rise. If you walk through the market, though, and speak to the traders and shoppers, you will start to understand how thin the strings are that are keeping the country together.

If you only see the streets of Juba from the window of a brand new Land Rover, you may think there is security in the city, too. The only people you will see brandishing weapons are the soldiers manning checkpoints or filling the backs of pick-up trucks. If you speak to those soldiers, though, you will find that, although they all wear one uniform, they are from two armies.

Thanks to the power-sharing agreement that was arranged to end the hostilities that started in 2013, the SPLA and the SPLA-IO (or In Opposition, Riek Machar's forces) both have armed forces in the capital. They look, to foreign eyes, like the same force, but they are in fact bitter enemies. For all the new construction, the new cars, and the well-wishing *kawaja*, Juba is a city made of tinder and full of sparks.

One day, on a street full of money-changers and their armed guards, I heard my name called from a late-model four-wheel drive. When I looked in the window of the car, I saw a man roughly my age who I recognised as Ajak Mayol Bior, one of my former comrades in arms.

I had not seen Ajak since I was chased from Ethiopia by the Eritreans, but I recognised his face instantly. We hugged, and Ajak started to cancel his appointments for the day.

Ajak took me to a coffee shop and, over macchiato, he told me about his life. He too was a lawyer. I knew the court system in South Sudan was a mess, but Ajak told me stories that verged on the absurd – of judges only being able to read and write Arabic, despite English being the official language of the court, of criminal cases mysteriously becoming civil cases mid-trial, of people being detained at the behest of the SPLA, and courts being compelled to bring charges (and convictions) later.

I was thirty-two and Ajak was only a few years older, but we swapped war stories and compared injuries like old men.

'Tell me, Deng, do you have any toenails?'

I didn't – it was a by-product of that long march from my village to Pinyudo.

'I have one,' he laughed. 'Hanging on, like a man on the edge of a cliff.'

We talked about the executions in Pinyudo. He remembered the occasion better than I did.

'Do you remember the doctor? You don't? He came in after the shooting to make sure the prisoners were all dead, but one was not. The doctor killed the man himself! To have children see such things – it was all too horrible.'

It was good to be with Ajak. He understood my past and I was awed by the fact that he had had the opportunity to live in Canada and yet decided to stay in Juba and attempt to make things better in our homeland.

After the coffees, I yearned to be next to the Nile again, and Ajak said he knew a place.

We went to a bar on the bank of the river, which was frequented by well-to-do locals, and *kawaja*. We put some plastic seats on the bank, and gin and tonics in our hands, and we looked at the river. To our left, some Bari tribesmen bathed naked, and to our right, the water diverted around a partially submerged troop transport that had been scuttled by Khartoum before the fall of the capital.

'Do you have nightmares, Deng?' Ajak asked me. I told him I did.

'I do not have any dreams anymore, but I know I am an unusual one.'

I asked Ajak how he managed to chase the bad dreams away.

'I don't sleep,' he said, chuckling. I don't know if he was joking or not.

Ajak and I talked about the future. We talked about the UN, and a compensation case he was considering taking on in which a drunk forklift driver on a UN base had caused a local woman to lose her legs. We mused on whether the case could be brought to a foreign court. We talked about the women in our lives, and our families, and the SPLA generals who we had fought with in the war who now ran the country.

We were of one mind, until we got onto the topic of the legal acknowledgement of the crimes that had been committed during the war. Ajak believed in amnesty and reconciliation councils, which had worked with some success in South Africa and the Democratic Republic of Congo. In those councils, culpability was recognised, but there was no sanction. I believed in nothing less than full prosecution. I thought of John, and the fact that I couldn't stomach knowing that his murderers would freely live in the same city as me.

I was full of verve when I spoke of trials and convictions, but Ajak would only meet my kinetic energy with a smile and soft words.

'My friend, I would love to see all the criminals behind bars too, but it simply isn't going to happen. And the effort could tear the country apart.'

That evening, I met with some old friends and family members in the restaurant of an Australian–Sudanese man who had left during the war and then joined the

Australian Defence Forces. The man had done multiple tours in Afghanistan, before moving back to Juba and setting up some businesses.

We drank scotch, and talked about football and politics, and eventually my brother, John. These men were some of John's closest friends in South Sudan, and I wanted to know more details about his death.

After John had told me he had been shot, he was out of contact, but I'd heard from the SPLA that he was safe, evacuated to the other side of the Nile. But then he was found dead.

That fact had always stuck, like a knot, in my stomach. When violence reigns in a place like South Sudan, it's not unusual for a certain type of person to take the opportunity to settle a score and attribute the death to war, and I had always wondered if John's bodyguards or fellow SPLA officers had actually killed him.

The men who I drank with that night could account for almost all of John's time, from when the fighting broke out to when his body was found by Akau. At the time of his death, John had been cut off from his unit, and the men were certain that he was with no compatriots when the Nuer militiamen killed him.

I said that still didn't account for the SPLA sources telling me many times that John was safe on the other side of the river. The men all spoke at once, telling me that that was a lie being told about almost all of the men injured in battles on the Nile. The SPLA had a civil war to prosecute, and was not interested in searching for bodies or lost soldiers, so that blanket lie was told of the injured and suspected dead.

As the night went on and I heard more and more, I lost my suspicions about the circumstances of John's death. His was just another killing unattached to his history or identity except as it related to his tribe. He was not the victim of a grand conspiracy; he was just another man who was burned up from the friction and heat created between the Dinka and the Nuer tribes.

'He loved you, Deng,' my uncle Philip Nyuon Akau said during a pause in the conversation.

'Then why did he beat me?' I asked. Philip instantly knew I was talking about the incident at the Ifo refugee camp when I'd refused to run from the Al-Shifta fighters, as he was in Eastern Kenya when it happened.

'He wanted to keep you alive and he didn't know any other way to get through to you. You were wild then. He cried after he did it,' Philip continued. 'And I think that was the only time I ever saw him cry.'

A few days later Ben and I flew from Juba to Bor in an old Cessna Grand Caravan, with the Nile to our right the

whole flight. It's always arresting to fly around South Sudan
– a country that's on the verge of famine and plagued by
fights over grazing rights – and see the seemingly endless
expanse of verdant ground.

We landed on the only straight stretch of bitumen in
the whole of Jonglei state. Move around Bor – and most of
South Sudan – and you notice that the benefits of international aid aren't spread evenly around the country. Juba is
the trough – the biggest and toughest pigs go there to dip
their snouts, and the rest of the country makes do with
what is left over.

Before heading into the village, we went into the market
in Bor town to buy supplies for my mother. There I found
the sacks of rice, beans, sugar and flour that I wanted,
but also stalls with AK-47s at less than forty dollars and
7.62 millimetre rounds at thirty cents each. Here in the
country, security is guaranteed by family and by tribe, not
by the state. I bought the supplies I needed and arranged
for a driver and car to take us and the sacks to my village.

As we drove past the huge United Nations Mission in
South Sudan (UNMISS) camp – a base that was overrun
in 2014 causing the death of thirty people – I was told
about a much more recent attack, which happened out
the front of the camp. Just a few days earlier, a group of
Murle raiders were on their way to kidnap some women and

children when they ran into an SPLA ambush. The SPLA soldiers calmly killed all the Murle, practically under the shadow of the UN flags. Things do not change in a place like South Sudan just because *kawaja* with blue helmets come to town.

When we arrived in the village of Malek, where my mother was living. I found her preparing food. She cried and shook with excitement when I opened the door of our vehicle. I had sent word I was coming but, with no electricity or telephone, it was impossible for her to know exactly when I would be arriving.

When I saw my mother, I felt a great sense of melancholy. I think most sons feel both joy and melancholy when they see their ageing mothers, but I was heavily weighted with the latter feeling. I later understood I felt that way because, with John dead, and me very much an Australian, South Sudan will not call to me at all once my mother passes away. I deeply care about the South Sudanese, and my family, and will always want to support them, but after my mother passes away, I'll do it from Australia.

There is little left for me in South Sudan, except my mother, and that is a sad thought for someone who sacrificed their childhood and fought a war for the country.

I spent some days in my village with my mother, as well as some other family members – including brothers and sisters who I barely knew. They were happy days, except when my mother asked me when I would be marrying. Her assumption was that I would marry a Dinka woman, but I'll not be marrying a Dinka woman. I will most likely be marrying an Australian woman. My mother knows nothing of Australian women, and I didn't have the heart to tell her that it's unlikely that any future Australian bride would be moving to South Sudan to join her and the other women in my village, as is our tradition.

When the time came to leave, it was a sad occasion. It always is, but this was a particularly tough moment. My mother is an old woman, and I don't know how many years she has left. This time, I felt added stress about when I would be able to journey back, due to the ongoing spectre of war, and also the reception of this book.

Before I ever return to Juba, I will have to weigh the response of the people who are named in this book to this account. People are killed in South Sudan for far less than the things I have revealed in these pages.

Before I left the village, my brother Akau joined me, as he was going to accompany me in the one task I wanted to undertake before leaving the country. Akau is an active serviceman in the SPLA but – like almost all civil servants in South Sudan – he had not been paid for more than two months. One of the many problems the current government has is one of liquidity, despite the country having abundant natural resources.

We drove past an abandoned oilfield, with the giant trucks that once traversed the site left in their tracks, empty and still since the 2013 fighting. That violence came as a surprise, and the foreign workers had to evacuate quickly. They had not returned, and all that could be looted from the site had been taken. We also drove past unused and overgrown vegetable fields. The local farmers had not planted anything because they didn't believe that their seed would become crops before they would be moved off their land by violence. Fighting is why the country is poor and hungry. There is no other reason.

There were burned-out cars, and even destroyed battle tanks on the side of the road. We stopped to take a photograph of one of the tanks and our driver warned us not to walk too far from the road.

'Mines?' I asked. I know some of the land between Bor and Juba had been littered with them.

'Not here,' he said. 'Bodies here.'

It seems many people tried to escape Bor via this road during the fighting in 2013, and were chased off the side of the road. Their bodies still lie rotting where they were killed.

We reached our destination, Goi – a small, dusty village that looked like any of the other villages on the Nile, except for two things – a very modern toilet block and, across a large playground, a long, thin modern one-storey building. It was a school that John had built. A school I'd heard him talk about sometimes after his businesses became successful, but had never seen.

It was all so John – John the aid worker, John the father, John the Dinka-Bor and John the scholar. John knew that the best national investment – both from a financial and cultural perspective – was primary schools. Co-educational primary schools.

I had no idea it was an institution of such size and relative modernity. There was no other building like it around the villages – let alone a school.

John had always appreciated the education he got from the Christian missionaries before he went to fight in the war. He appreciated what he learned then, but more than that, he appreciated how it gave him a perspective outside of the Nile and the war. That perspective had dragged me into the life I now lead. It was John who had conceived the idea of a life outside of South Sudan, and it was he who imagined an educated life in Australia, also. He was the one who spurred us into higher education, and I know that much of my reality is his unrealised dreams.

One of John's realised dreams was this school. A dream that lived for a couple of years, and then died, with him and the fighting of 2013. The school now lies empty.

There was almost no one left in Goi, but a woman Akau knew appeared as we arrived and led us to a mound of dirt next to the school. Akau dropped to his knees in front of the dirt, and I joined him. John's body lay under that mound.

I have seen a lot of death in my life. I have seen bodies, and many times I have seen the moment when life becomes death, but the thought of John being under that mound, not hustling and working and planning and living, disgusted me. I still don't know how to process John's death.

I rubbed my palms on the mound of dirt and I could feel John. I could feel his whole life. I could feel all the fear and pain he'd experienced in the war. I could feel the hope and exhilaration he'd felt when escaping the war, and Kakuma, and the mounting, crushing frustration of the realisation that life in Australia was to be complicated and difficult in a very different way. I could also feel his exhilaration at the school opening. His love of Elizabeth and his children ran through me too.

I had expected John to be a perfect man, and he had not been, and since I had been a boy, I had resented that. Now I felt his imperfections as a necessary by-product of his experiences and nature. He could be nothing but what he is – what he was. It was all John. In retrospect, I saw John wholly, and loved him. Tears welled in my eyes – the first that had ever come for my brother.

I wanted to give John something as he had given me so much. I took my shirt off and buried it in the dirt. I wanted to return what he had once given me. As was the case when he gave me his shirt, it was just a gesture, and it meant nothing but perhaps: 'we are brothers'.

EPILOGUE

Four weeks after I returned from South Sudan, I was fidgeting with a glass of beer at an event at the New South Wales Art Gallery celebrating the Archibald Prize. There were fine people around – artists and their subjects, and also sponsors and financiers. The portrait of me didn't win the Archibald Prize – instead a portrait of Barry Humphries took the award – but I was invited to speak at the awards announcement. I spoke a little about myself, and Nick's painting. I would have liked Nick to have won, but I don't know enough about art to know whether he should have or not. He seemed happy, anyway. I was in a decent mood, also.

Less than forty-eight hours earlier, Juba had been echoing with the sounds of gunfire and artillery. The fighting started after an argument at a checkpoint, which escalated into a pitched battle, eventually bringing tanks, artillery pieces and helicopter gunships into the capital. One of the compounds I was in while Ben and I were in Juba was overrun and now sits in ruins. The city is accounting for the dead. Hundreds of people have been killed but all of the people I care about in South Sudan are accounted for and a ceasefire appears to be holding. That is what we get to hope for in South Sudan – that when the violence happens, the people that we love all stay alive, and so I was in a decent mood.

After my Archibald speech, I sat down to a smattering of polite applause. As I often did after speaking in public, I felt like I had added further to a ledger detailing the debt I have to the people who I share my story with. I have benefited from the misery of Kapoeta, Pinyudo and Kakuma, but they have not.

I have gained status, and opportunity, and all they get is more difficulty. There is no way of knowing what state South Sudan will be in when you read these words. As I write, the country is broke, the two men in charge are bitter rivals and there are 4.8 million people on the verge of starvation. Also, most of the *kawaja* are outside of the

South Sudanese borders, having been chased away by the most recent fighting.

As I sat at my table at the art gallery, and nibbled at my entree, I thought of all the luck in my life. I was born lucky, and I stayed lucky, even as circumstance and war ruined those around me. There was polite conversation around the table and someone asked about the recent fighting. I shook my head and said: 'Very sad, very sad.'

For all the luck in my life, I know I must pay back great debts. Do I owe a debt to Australia? I look at my life and I say of course I do. Do I owe a debt to the African diaspora, too? I think the answer is again yes, because it's there I think I am best positioned to offer help. The more difficult question is whether I owe a debt to South Sudan.

That country sent me into military slavery, threw me against the grind of a bloody war, and killed my brother. The country is a near-bankrupt kleptocracy ruled by demagogues and madmen. Do I owe a debt to all that?

I turned thirty-three years of age this week, but I feel like a much older man than that. I feel as though I have lived three lives. I have lived as a Dinka, ruled by custom and the big god *Nhialic*. I have lived life as a soldier ruled by maniacs and death. I have also lived life as an Australian, and law, justice and reason rule that life.

That last life is my true life, and the one I choose to continue. I am more an Australian, and more a lawyer than I am a soldier or Dinka, but I will also forever be South Sudanese. My skin will never change, and I shall never completely lose my accent. If I ever see the Nile again, and eagles soaring above it, my heart will skip a beat, no matter how old or grey I may be. My mother will always be my mother, my brother always my brother.

Also this week, I set up the board for the charitable foundation that will exist in John Mac's name. It's taken me some time to bring the foundation to life, in no small part because I couldn't figure out who the beneficiaries of the foundation should be.

I have now decided that the foundation in John Mac's name must benefit the nation he was inexorably tied to and undoubtedly loved. The foundation will also be dedicated to that which John and I received in Australia, but were denied in South Sudan, and were, respectively, most passionate about – education and justice.

The foundation will provide mentoring and scholarships for refugees who wish to go to an Australian university. There will also be a focus on the transition from university to the workplace – the place where John had such difficulty.

The foundation will also attempt to reopen the school that John built in Goi. I can think of no better way of

memorialising John, but this goal will be far more complicated than the first. The spectre of war, and tribal hatred,
will threaten to derail our efforts at any moment but we,
as John did, can only try.

The third goal may be the most difficult of all, however.
We will attempt to bring justice to South Sudan.

I want disputes over resources in the land of my birth
settled in court. I want the rule of law, not gun rule to be
what defines South Sudanese politics. I also want to see
those who feast on the resources and lives of South Sudan
for their own personal benefit sit in the dock.

How can the foundation help in those efforts? We
empower men like Ajak with the legal resources required
to fight injustice. I have twice become intoxicated on the
power of compassionate but codified order – first when
learning the law of the Dinka, and then when learning
the law of Australia. I think the people of South Sudan
deserve the opportunity to be similarly enraptured, but at
the moment they have little opportunity because the legal
system is in disarray, and very few people understand what
the rules in South Sudan are, or why they are in place.

The foundation will set up a link between Australia and
the University of Juba, so that people like Ajak can defend
themselves with legal precedent when facing injustice. There
will be times when those protections will be meagre against

the violence, but in the quiet months perhaps a framework of justice may be built. Perhaps a passion for justice and reason may take hold. At the very least, we must try.

I will leave you with this thought: I believe there are really only two things to do in life – find things you believe in, and then dedicate yourself to them. That's why I have a deep hatred for both apathy and tribalism, as apathy robs you of your ability to try, and tribalism steals your ability to find the things you believe in.

Tribalism is also one of the few ways that one human can look at another and, knowing nothing about them, see them as lesser.

I believe in justice and education, but I also believe that all people, including refugees, should be recognised as the people that they are. My hope is that this book has helped you believe the same. Perhaps the songs of my life have had a different tone and cadence to yours, but they are about love and hope and yearning and sadness, just like yours.

My hope is that now you know my songs, perhaps one day, when you see my brother, you will also see yours.

AFTERWORD

The first draft of this book was finished two weeks ago, and my thoughts about my identity and nation were settled. I was Australian, and reconciled with the fact that I might never again set foot in the country of my birth. Then, a week ago, I was drawn back into the South Sudanese morass.

I was in Parramatta court when I got the call. It was from my brother Akau.

'Brother, we are in the bush.'

Being 'in the bush' means something very specific in South Sudan. It means you have been chased away, and it often means you are being hunted. It means you have a weapon, and it also usually means you are preparing for retaliation.

Akau explained that a Dinka-Bor clan called the Gwala had used the recent instability and fighting as a moment of opportunity, attacking my village so they could steal cattle, loot stores and also take over nearby fertile land.

Akau and some of the other men tried to resist the attack, but the Gwala came with PK machine guns and grenades. The men of the village ran into the bush with their weapons, but they had no ammunition for a counterattack. I asked Akau where my family was; where my mother was. Most of my close family members were accounted for – either in Bor or in the bush – except for my mother. She and the other elders were being held hostage by the Gwala, to discourage a counterattack.

I went home and started doing all that I could to get her released. I still have contacts in the SPLA, and implored them to go to my village and free her. There was nothing they could do. Not only were they reluctant to get involved in a clan conflict, rain had been falling for the previous four days and the road to Malek was impassable for their vehicles. I spoke to all the family members I could, to see what leverage they could use to free my mother. They said there was nothing they could do.

The situation could not be resolved, or not from Australia anyway. I became increasingly frantic, and the thought of my mother being held by that clan against her wishes lived in my every moment. I couldn't sleep, or work, or eat. I dreaded the call telling me that she was dead.

A call did come, and it was from my mother. A phone had been smuggled to the elders who were being held at the leper colony next to the village. My mother wanted to call me to let me know that she was alive. I asked her about her health and the state of the village. Her house – a house I had paid for – had been burned down, and her granddaughter, my late brother Adut's daughter, was missing. My mother and the other elders were being kept with no food, no blankets and no mosquito nets. I could hear the fear, but also resolve in her voice. I told her I would get her out. She told me she didn't want to leave.

'I can't leave my village. I can't leave my family.'

The more calls I made, the more it became obvious that the SPLA were not going to intervene in the matter for us, and I even found out that some of my tribe had been arrested for the death of a Gwala tribesman killed in the assault. Such is the nature of South Sudan. The rule of law is only applied when it suits the people holding the levers of power, and it seemed that those holders were siding with the Gwala.

I couldn't stand being in Sydney. I had flat whites and Ubers, friends and safe streets and billable hours, and none of it meant anything to me while I knew that my mother was sick, and being held at gunpoint. I had to go back to South Sudan.

I booked a ticket to Juba, and my friends and colleagues lined up to explain to me why it was a bad idea. Their arguments varied initially, but all funnelled into one protestation: 'What happened to John will happen to you.'

It didn't matter. I started to understand the motivation that drove John's fateful decision. I couldn't live my happy, comfortable life knowing that my mother's life was in the balance. Not when I could potentially do something about it. Potential mortal danger was not as potent a motivator as the thought of loved ones in peril.

My counter-argument to my friends and colleagues was: 'What would you do if it was your mother?'

I started to plan my trip. When I got to Juba I would meet with General Kuol Manyang Juuk, who was the highest-ranking SPLA official that I could get in front of, and make my pitch. If he couldn't or wouldn't help, I would work my way down the SPLA line.

If the SPLA were not going to intervene and quickly, I would fly up to Bor, and there I would petition the governor. If that didn't work, then I would join Akau, and figure out a more practical solution. Men and weapons can be purchased in South Sudan very cheaply and the only justice that exists in that country is that which you can leverage yourself.

I abhor clan violence, and had no desire to be dragged into or possibly even fuel a clan war, but I had to get my mother and her family members free. I could think of nothing else.

I told an Australian army officer stationed at the nearby UNMISS base about my plans to help my mother. He was aware of the conflict, and while the UN mandate strictly forbade intervention, he said he would have a UN patrol stop in the village and see if they could come back with my mother. After the UN patrol I found that my mother was now allowed to leave, but that she wouldn't budge until all of her family members were accounted for.

The night before my flight I arranged a large sum of hard currency, for use in case all other avenues were exhausted. Then, just before going to bed, I got a call from an uncle saying he was with my mother in Bor. He was on my mother's side of the family and neither from my clan nor the Gwala, and had managed to account for all the lost family members, and arranged for the Gwala to agree to the release of all the elders. He also told me that the village had been completely destroyed. Everything that could be looted had been, and everything that wasn't useful had been burned. I cancelled my flight and sent my contingency cash to Bor to buy supplies, food and medicine.

I was in court the day I was supposed to fly, and then in court the next day, and the day after that. I made myself available again for speaking engagements, and met with those who were helping me set up the John Mac Foundation. An Australian life goes on for me, and a South Sudanese life goes on for them.

As I write this, my mother is currently squatting in Bor, crying for a home that no longer exists; my brother is in the bush with his weapon in his hand and revenge on his mind; my family is scattered, my village is gone and I have no idea what their future is.

I am in a Redfern pub having a pale ale, thinking about how the past can never completely be archived. Especially when the songs of your past are sung in the tongues of South Sudan.

ACKNOWLEDGEMENTS

Deng:

Thank you to Elizabeth, George, Joshua and the rest of my family who have accompanied me on this journey. I'm grateful to my dear friends Joe Correy, Caroline Ayling, Lamin Colley and Mickey Negus.

For the guidance I thank Hugh Riminton, Dr Michael Adams, Hon. Terry Buddin SC and Hugh Selby. A big shout out to everyone at Western Sydney University, my colleagues in the legal profession, Vanessa and Lydia and the team at Hachette, Sally McPherson, my Australian Mum Felicity Bennett-Bremner and, of course, to Christine and Bob Harrison. And finally, thank you to my co-writer Ben Mckelvey: it was a wild ride, mate, and I couldn't have done it with anyone but you!

Ben:

I'd like to thank Elizabeth, Hugh, Vanessa and Peggy for their invaluable help in Australia, and Ajak, Philip, and Mikeyas for their essential support in Africa. Most of all I'd like to thank Deng, who managed to bring light to even the darkest corners of this story.

A portion of the proceeds from *Songs of a War Boy* will go to the John Mac Foundation to further education and justice in Australia and South Sudan.

I am very proud that I have been able to set up a charitable foundation in my brother's name. I want his name, and his life, to stand for something despite his sudden death. If John was alive today, he would be making the world a better place. With the establishment of this foundation, he still is.

In Australia, we will provide scholarships to enable people from refugee backgrounds to go to university. We will support people whose lives have been interrupted by war make it into higher education, hang in there, and once completed, make the successful transition into meaningful employment. It was this last transition that John struggled with, which ultimately led to his life being lost.

In South Sudan, we will support criminal and environmental justice, by making resources available to the people who are fighting the good fight. Students, lawyers, judges and educators – by arming them with books, scholarships and new skills, they will be able to hold people accountable for war crimes. Crimes which, to this day, have not been answered for.

To learn more or become involved, please visit our website:
www.johnmacfoundation.org

Thank you,

hachette
AUSTRALIA

If you would like to find out more about Hachette Australia,
our authors, upcoming events and new releases you can visit
our website, Facebook or follow us on Twitter:

hachette.com.au
facebook.com/HachetteAustralia
twitter.com/HachetteAus